THE
JONATHAN
PARABLES

ELSA PAPULOT

BALBOA.
PRESS

A DIVISION OF HAY HOUSE

Balboa Press books may be ordered through booksellers or by contacting:

Balboa Press
A Division of Hay House
1663 Liberty Drive
Bloomington, IN 47403
www.balboapress.com
1 (877) 407-4847

Because of the dynamic nature of the Internet, any web addresses or links contained in this book may have changed since publication and may no longer be valid. The views expressed in this work are solely those of the author and do not necessarily reflect the views of the publisher, and the publisher hereby disclaims any responsibility for them.

The author of this book does not dispense medical advice or prescribe the use of any technique as a form of treatment for physical, emotional, or medical problems without the advice of a physician, either directly or indirectly. The intent of the author is only to offer information of a general nature to help you in your quest for emotional and spiritual well-being. In the event you use any of the information in this book for yourself, which is your constitutional right, the author and the publisher assume no responsibility for your actions.

Any people depicted in stock imagery provided by Thinkstock are models, and such images are being used for illustrative purposes only. Certain stock imagery © Thinkstock.

Print information available on the last page.

ISBN: 978-1-5043-3939-1 (sc)
ISBN: 978-1-5043-3941-4 (hc)
ISBN: 978-1-5043-3940-7 (e)

Library of Congress Control Number: 2015913520

Balboa Press rev. date: 08/18/2015

"*I have also spoken to the prophets, and I gave them numerous visions, and through the prophets I gave Parables.*" --- *Hosea 12: 10*

"*When there is a prophet among you, I, the LORD, reveal myself to them in visions, I speak to them in dreams.*" --- *Numbers 12: 6*

PARABLE I

Solomon

"Pay attention, Jonathan, or you'll miss the question!"

The girl seemed to be very concerned for her friend. Her friend didn't appear to be concerned at all. He sat in the class room, acting as though he hadn't a care in the world. **But down in his knowing place – the place no other person, most times even himself, was allowed to visit – he was afraid...or at the very least he was unsure of himself.**

The teacher was a woman. She was elegant; she was confident; she was patient; she was graceful; she was, in every sense, regal. She was all the things Jonathan was not.

"Each of you will be taking an individual oral test," the teacher explained. "You will each be given one question. The test is Pass or Fail. You will either Pass the test or Fail the test, depending on your answer."

Jonathan continued to act as though he was not concerned. He continued to act as though he didn't have any doubt in his ability. He acted. He had become very good at acting. Now twenty-four years old, the lines between reality and the act were becoming blurred even to himself. He didn't visit his knowing place very often. *And still, his friend was concerned:*

"Pay attention, Jonathan, or you'll miss the question," she implored again, to no avail.

And the test began. The teacher went around the room, asking each student their individual question. Jonathan didn't hear any of the other students' questions. He was too busy maintaining the façade of confidence and nonchalance. All the while, his friend pleaded with him to pay attention.

And then it was his turn. He was terrified, but could never let on. The teacher asked the question: "Who was Solomon?"

Jonathan was so busy constructing the mask – and internally fighting off his feeling of unbridled fear – that he misheard the question. "Which one?" he asked.

The teacher looked at him with a puzzled expression. His friend just shook her head; not in disgust, but out of genuine concern.

"Which one what?" the teacher asked.

"Which Saul do you mean?" he said, doing his best to sell the act. "Do you mean King Saul or Saul of Tarsus?"

"No," she said. "The question is, 'Who was Solomon?'"

"Oh, that's easy," he said, pretending to know the answer. But he was so deep into the act by this point, the momentum carried him along. "He was our first great King."

The answer just hung out there, suspended in mid-air. It stopped the teacher in her tracks. She was completely caught off guard. She considered the answer; she obviously hadn't expected this reply. And Jonathan secretly anguished over his fate. **He knew, in his knowing place, which he was thrust into because of the enormity of the situation, that he really didn't know who Solomon was.** *He waited for the ax to fall. A strange look came to the teacher's face, as though some illumination had occurred.*

"I'll accept that answer," she said.

Jonathan, though maintaining his air of confidence to the outsiders **(and all people were outsiders, really),** *felt shame in his knowing place, because he had not been honest: he didn't really know the answer, but he passed the test regardless.*

The first truly coherent thought that came to his mind after waking was this: "David was our first great King, not Solomon."

After recounting the dream to his priest, Father Thomas, the man of God gave him three points to consider. "First," the robust holy man said, "The question is always more important than the answer. Second, you must take the time to find out how Solomon failed. And third, you mustn't forget that for whatever reason, you passed the test. You must discover why your answer was accepted."

As Jonathan left the holy man's office, Raphael sat watching. The Healing Angel, one of the seven archangels who sit in the presence of God, watched the young man. And he watched The Almighty. And he waited. When would The Creator send him to earth again? What would the next message be? When would he receive his next assignment?

Meanwhile, Jonathan was left to discover the meaning of the dream. Who was Solomon? And how is he our first great King?

Even a Biblical novice knows that Solomon was the wisest – and richest – King who ever lived. Novice though he was, Jonathan knew there was much more to the question of who Solomon was. And being the richest – or the wisest – wouldn't make Solomon great in God's economy. And to this point, Jonathan was not familiar at all with how Solomon failed. And thus the journey of enlightenment began. Would Jonathan have embarked on the journey had he known what Raphael knew? The Healing Angel waited, and watched, and pondered the knowledge he was given by The Almighty: it was going to take twenty-seven years for Jonathan to unravel the message. Raphael watched as his charge began a quest for the Holy Grail. Not a quest in search of some mysterious chalice that held magical powers; not a quest in a land of sorcerers or knights who wield magical swords pulled out of a stone. Jonathan's quest was real and he was, although unbeknownst to himself, set upon a journey in search of the true Grail. Only this was not a legend, this was real life.

Jonathan never thought of himself as a hero, but his life was about to become heroic, though he would, until the very end, think himself cursed. His life was about to become the embodiment of Joseph Campbell's definition of the hero: *"Many visionaries, and even leaders and heroes are close to the edge of being neurotic. And so it must be. They've moved out of the society that would have protected them, and into the Dark Forest, into the world of Fire, of original experience. Original experience has not been interpreted for you, and you've got to work out your life for yourself. Either you can take it or you can't. You don't have to go far off the interpreted path to find yourself in very difficult situations. The courage to face the trials and to bring a whole new body of possibilities into the field of interpreted experience for other people to experience – that is the hero's deed."* [1]

Most people live lives they've seen lived before. That's the natural process and order of human life on earth. And most of these people have the benefit, as they navigate through these lives, of relying on what they've seen others do when they get to the rough spots in the road. But some people, like Jonathan, find themselves in a life they have not seen lived before. And they have to navigate through the valleys using their own intuition. Those who watch from the outside of such lives watch the misfits flail to and fro as they forge a new experience. Those who watch from the outside look on with sympathy and sometimes even pity as they watch the misfits thrash and suffer, wondering why the lost soul doesn't simply take the beaten path – the path that has been tested and found true time and time again. And the fumbling fledglings ask the same question themselves, truly not knowing why their path just won't follow the same road map of their content counterparts.

And so it came to pass that Jonathan set out to find King Solomon. Not because his occupation or pursued degree demanded it, but because it was the message he received one Christmas Eve night long ago. He did it because it was the personal dream he believed God had given him. Strangely enough, he did it because it was the only thing in his life that really made sense – in his knowing place. To people of his own culture, he would be seen as an idealist, or irresponsible, or naïve, and maybe even a little daft. But something in Jonathan's DNA empowered him with the knowledge that the Hebrew word for "dream" is *chalom,* which means: *"to be made strong or whole."* And also, somewhere in his spirit was the encouragement passed through the ages by the natives of America, which says, *"The dream is real; follow the dream."* So he did the only thing he was capable of, foolish or not. He followed the dream, and instead of a Technicolor Dream Coat woven by his father, he carried with him the neurotic-plated sword of Don Quixote.

Solomon was the child of King David and Bathsheba. After performing such feats as defeating Goliath the Philistine, and subsequently winning many other victories in battle, David succeeded in uniting the kingdom of Israel and sat securely on the throne. Perhaps it is the normal human tendency to become overconfident in one's own ability that had settled on David, when after defeating the Arameans he decided that spring, "when kings normally go out to war," that he would send Joab in his place with the Israelite army "to fight the Ammonites" (2 Samuel 11: 1).

In his current feeling of invincibility, perhaps he became complacent spiritually, which caused him to indulge in idleness. "Late one afternoon, after his midday rest, David got out of bed and was walking on the roof of the palace. As he looked out over the city, he noticed a woman of unusual beauty taking a bath. He sent someone to find out who she was, and he was told, 'She is Bathsheba, the daughter of Eliam and wife of Uriah the Hittite'" (2 Samuel 11: 2, 3).

David, overcome with lust, sent messengers to get her; "and when she came to the palace, he slept with her" (2 Samuel 11: 4). So the King of Israel, the man God himself said was "a man after my own heart," had committed adultery with the wife of one of his officers. Not long after the transgression, Bathsheba sent word to David that she was pregnant.

A man in David's position has several courses of action available to him in this situation. David chose to send word to Joab: "Send me Uriah the Hittite" (2 Samuel 11: 6). Surely, one might think, David is going to confess his sin and ask forgiveness.

What David does instead, however, is instruct Uriah to go home, hoping of course that his soldier will take the natural course of action and sleep with his wife, Bathsheba. Uriah, however, did not go home, but instead slept at the palace entrance with the King's guard. "When David heard that Uriah had not gone home, he summoned him and asked, 'What's the matter? Why didn't you go home last night after being away for so long?'

"Uriah replied, 'The Ark and the armies of Israel and Judah are living in tents, and Joab and my master's men are camping in the open fields. How could I go home to wine and dine and sleep with my wife? I swear that I would never do such a thing'" (2 Samuel 11: 10, 11).

At some point, after David had emerged from the enchanted mist which currently clouded his faculties, he must have felt a sting of pain with the realization that a Hittite acted more honorably in God's sight than did the anointed King of Israel. But at the moment, his carnal instincts guided him. David took efforts to conceal his sin even further. "David invited him to dinner and got him drunk. But even then he couldn't get Uriah to go home to his wife. Again he slept at the palace entrance with the King's palace guard" (2 Samuel 11: 13).

Now in a state of desperation, David writes a letter for Uriah to deliver to Joab. "The letter instructed Joab, 'Station Uriah on the front lines where the battle is fiercest. Then pull back so that he will be killed'" (2 Samuel 11: 15). So Joab follows David's orders and Uriah is killed. When Bathsheba hears the news, she mourns the death of her husband. "When the period of mourning was over, David sent for her and brought her to the palace, and she became one of his wives. Then she gave birth to a son. But the Lord was displeased with what David had done" (2 Samuel 11: 27).

But David had removed himself so far from the presence of God that he could not hear the rebuke from the Heavenly Father. But God, true to his word, continued to pursue the child he loved. God sent the prophet Nathan to bring David back to his senses. After Nathan has confronted David with his sin, the King of Israel confesses to the prophet, "I have sinned against the Lord" (2 Samuel 12: 13).

Nathan then delivers God's message to the King: "Yes, but the Lord has forgiven you, and you won't die for this sin (the Law called for adulterers to be stoned to death, but even though David lived under the Old Testament, he lived a New Testament life, proving the word of the Lord in Hosea 6: 6 – "For I desire mercy, not sacrifice."). Nevertheless, because you have shown utter contempt for the word of the Lord by doing this, your child will die" (2 Samuel 12: 14).

Although David had already been forgiven, and not experienced the consequences of the Law, he is nevertheless disciplined severely, once again proving that God is always true to his word: "My son, do not despise the Lord's discipline and do not resent his rebuke, because the Lord disciplines those he loves, and he punishes the son he delights in" (Proverbs 3: 11,

12). **God punished David because he delighted in him. And God punishes all those he accepts as his children. And he punishes each one individually according to that child's temperament and according to what that individual will respond to. And the purpose of God's discipline is always to mold his children into the image of Jesus, his only begotten son, who existed before the creation of the world.** "Our fathers disciplined us for a little while as they thought best; but God disciplines us for our good, that we may share in his holiness. No discipline seems pleasant at the time, but painful. Later on, however, it produces a harvest of righteousness and peace for those who have been trained by it" (Hebrews 12: 10, 11).

When the deadly illness came to David's son, he begged God to spare the life of his child. He refused to eat and laid all night on the bare ground. On the seventh day (seven being the number of completion) the child dies. The servants are hesitant to inform David of his child's death for fear that he might kill himself. When David discovers the truth, however, he surprisingly gets up and washes himself. He then puts lotion on and changes his clothes. He then goes to the Tabernacle and worships the Lord. After that, he goes to the palace and eats.

"His advisors were amazed. 'We don't understand you,' they told him. 'While the child was still living, you wept and refused to eat. But now that the child is dead, you have stopped your mourning and are eating again.'

"David replied, 'I fasted and wept while the child was alive for I said, 'Perhaps the Lord will be gracious to me and let the child live.' But why should I fast when he is dead? Can I bring him back again? I will go to him one day, but he cannot return to me'" (2 Samuel 12: 21-23).

Amazingly, David was able to actually *feel* forgiven. After the punishment had run its course, he wasted no time beating himself up or wallowing in self-pity. He accepts the discipline,

endures the discipline, and then moves on. A powerful example. God never said David was perfect – or ever expected him to be – he said that David was a man after his own heart. As David moves on from the discipline, he also carries with him a lesson truly learned. He is changed for the better and changed for good. A powerful example of one who loves God and who bathes in the sweet, sweet grace of God...while living under the Old Testament.

"Then David comforted Bathsheba, his wife, and slept with her. She became pregnant and gave birth to a son, and David named him Solomon. <u>The Lord loved the child and sent word through Nathan the prophet that they should name him Jedidiah (which means "beloved of the Lord")</u>, as the Lord had commanded" (2 Samuel 12: 24, 25). God is not vindictive; forgiveness is placing the transgression in the sea of forgetfulness, forgiveness means removing the sin "as far as the East is from the West." Start at any point on earth and begin walking west. You can walk from now to the end of time, and you will at no point ever begin to travel east. When the time of discipline had been completed for David, God blessed the union conceived in sin with a son who would become the most famous King in the world.

And God had grand plans for David's son. David sets his heart on building a Temple for the Ark of the Lord's covenant, which means he wanted to build a permanent dwelling place for the Lord's presence, a home for God's Holy Spirit. But God sends word through Nathan that it is not David, but his son Solomon who will build the Temple.

But before David dies, he makes sure Solomon will succeed in building the Lord's Temple. "David said, 'My son Solomon is still young and inexperienced. And since the Temple to be built for the Lord must be a magnificent structure, famous and glorious throughout the world, I will begin making preparations for it now.' So David collected vast amounts of building materials before his death" (1 Chronicles 22: 5).

When the materials for the Temple are collected, David sends for his son and explains the Lord's desire. David instructs Solomon to build a Temple for the Lord God of Israel, saying, "My son, I wanted to build a Temple to honor the name of the Lord my God. But the Lord said to me, 'You have killed many men in the battles you have fought. And since you have shed so much blood in my sight, you will not be the one to build a Temple to honor my name. <u>But you will have a son who will be a man of peace. I will give him peace with his enemies in all the surrounding lands. His name will be Solomon, and I will give peace and quiet to Israel during his reign. He is the one who will build a Temple to honor my name. He will be my son, and I will be his father. And I will secure the throne of his kingdom over Israel forever</u>'" (1 Chronicles 22: 7-10).

When the time had come, "David summoned all the officials to Jerusalem – the leaders of the tribes, the commanders of the army divisions, the other generals and captains, the overseers of the royal property and livestock, the palace officials, the mighty men, and all the brave warriors in the kingdom. David rose to his feet sand said, 'My brothers and my people! It was my desire to build a temple where the Ark of the Lord's Covenant, God's footstool, could rest permanently. I made the necessary preparations for building it, <u>but God said to me, 'You must not build a temple to honor my name, for you are a warrior and have shed much blood.</u>'

"Yet the Lord, the God of Israel has chosen me from among my father's family to be king over Israel forever. For he has chosen the tribe of Judah to rule, and from among the families of Judah he chose my father's family. And from my father's sons the Lord was pleased to make me king over all Israel. <u>And from among my sons – and the Lord has given me many – he chose</u>

Solomon to succeed me on the throne of Israel and to rule over the Lord's kingdom. He said to me, **'Your son Solomon will build my Temple and its courtyards,** *for I have chosen him as my son, and I will be his father.* **And if he continues to obey my commands and regulations** *as he does now,* **I will make his kingdom last forever.'"** (1 Chronicles 28: 1-7).

David then turns to Solomon and addresses him personally, saying, "And Solomon, my son, learn to know the God of your ancestors intimately." **God can be known by us intimately, but it happens over time, and it only happens with our purposeful intention and action. David says: "LEARN to know God INTIMATELY." It can only be done with our active intention. David continues:** "Worship and serve him with your whole heart and a willing mind." **If we ever expect to know God intimately, instead of just superficially, we must do three things: we must WORSHIP and SERVE with our whole heart; and the third directive is not as easy as it may sound at first - we must have a WILLING mind. We cannot worship or serve or obey the Lord out of compulsion, but from a willing mind. "For the Lord sees every heart and knows every plan and thought"** (1 Chronicles 28: 9).

David then gives Solomon a word of encouragement, followed by a warning: "If you seek him, you will find him (encouragement). But if you forsake him, he will reject you forever (warning). So take this seriously. The Lord has chosen you to build a Temple as his sanctuary. Be strong, and do the work" (1 Chronicles 28: 9, 10). It is something to be taken seriously, building the Temple for the Lord's sanctuary; and we are the Lord's temple if we have faith in Jesus, which should also be taken seriously.

And Solomon enjoyed amazing success as the new king. "They crowned David's son Solomon as their new king. They anointed him before the Lord as their leader, and they anointed

Zadok as priest. So Solomon took the throne of the Lord in the place of his father, David, <u>and he succeeded in everything, and all Israel obeyed him.</u> All the officials, the warriors, and the sons of King David pledged their loyalty to King Solomon. <u>And the Lord exalted Solomon in the sight of all Israel, and he gave Solomon greater royal splendor than any king in Israel before him</u>" (1 Chronicles 29: 22-25).

***

To this point, Jonathan had found what made Solomon great, but nothing of how Solomon failed. The search for the Grail had only just begun for the real-life knight, or would he instead turn out to be a knight-errant? It remained to be seen at this point whether Jonathan would proceed to become a modern-day Sir Galahad or just another well-intentioned Don Quixote. So he trudged on, and on. At times he felt close to God, as though he were on the highest peak of the mountain. There were also moments, even seasons, when he believed he was forgotten by The Creator – not by the will of God, but because of his utter weakness and depravity. But always, whether by his own volition - or the nudging of the Source of Immortality – he found his way back to the journey, and trudged. He felt a kinship, though not voluntarily, with Hawthorne's character in **_The House of the Seven Gables_**: *"Persons who have wandered, or been expelled, out of the common track of things, even were it for a better system, desire nothing so much as to be led back. They shiver in their loneliness, be it on a mountain-top or in a dungeon. Now, Phoebe's presence made a home about her – that very sphere which the outcast, the prisoner, the wretch beneath mankind, the wretch aside from it, or the wretch above it, instinctively pines after – a home!...At his highest elevation, the poet needs no human intercourse; but he finds it dreary to descend, and be a stranger."*[2]

Jonathan felt many times as though he were an outcast, a prisoner, and a wretch aside from mankind. There were times he even felt he was the wretch below mankind. And oh how his heart pined for that sister of Phoebe who could give him a home. So he trudged, seeking the Grail, seeking the answer to the questions: Who was Solomon and how did Solomon fail? And why, if he failed, was he – instead of David - our first great King?

Solomon began his tenure on the throne of Israel very well. And he pleased God very much. And God appeared to Solomon in a dream one night. The Lord said, "What do you want? Ask, and I will give it to you" (2 Chronicles 1: 7). *The origin of the genie in the bottle, who grants a wish to the one who frees him, can be traced back to a legend about Solomon. According to the legend, Solomon trapped a type of demon, known as a "Jinn" in a magical bottle. The singular form of "jinn" is "jinnee."*

"Solomon replied to God, 'You showed great and faithful love to David, my father *(God's love for David was GREAT and FAITHFUL)*, and now you have made me king in his place. O Lord God, please continue to keep your promise to David, my father *(God's promise was to David, not Solomon)*, for you have made me king over a people as numerous as the dust of the earth! Give me the wisdom and knowledge to lead them properly, for who could possibly govern this great people of yours?'" (2 Chronicles 1: 8-10).

"God said to Solomon, 'Because your greatest desire is to help your people, and you did not ask for wealth, riches, fame, or even the death of your enemies or a long life *(all things that someone who had found a genie in a bottle would ask for)*, but rather you asked for wisdom and knowledge to properly govern my people – I will certainly give you the wisdom and knowledge you requested. But I will also give you wealth, riches, and fame

such as no king had before you or will ever have in the future!'"
(2 Chronicles 1: 11, 12).

Solomon's reign began so well. He pleased the Lord greatly.
We know Solomon today as the "wisest and richest king who
ever lived." He is given credit for being the author of Proverbs.
But that was a byproduct of the character that had pleased
God. When told he could have anything he wanted, his heart's
desire was to have wisdom and knowledge in order to govern
God's people well.

How did Solomon fail? And if he failed, why is he our first
great king?

When Solomon had finished building the Temple, he
offered prayers of dedication. When Solomon had finished the
dedication, "the Lord appeared to Solomon a second time, as he
had done before at Gibeon. The Lord said to him, 'I have heard
your prayer and your petition. I have set this Temple apart to be
holy – this place you have built where my name will be honored
forever. I will always watch over it, for it is dear to my heart'"
(1 Kings 9: 2, 3).

So far, so good. Solomon went on to accomplish many
things and he astonished the people with his wise rulings. Israel
enjoyed the zenith of its prosperity during Solomon's reign.

But Solomon failed.

*"Now King Solomon loved many foreign women. Besides Pharaoh's
daughter, he married women from Moab, Ammon, Edom, Sidon, and
from among the Hittites. <u>The Lord had clearly instructed the people of
Israel, 'You must not marry them, because they will turn your hearts to
their gods.' Yet Solomon insisted on loving them anyway</u>. He had 700
wives of royal birth and 300 concubines. And in fact, they did turn his
heart away from the Lord"* (1 Kings 11: 1-3).

When God talks about foreign women in the Old Testament,
he is talking about people who worship other gods instead of
the One True God. These people are referred to as *"unbelievers"*

in the New Testament. So Solomon's failure began with his marrying unbelievers - whom God had specifically commanded the Israelites not to marry - who turned his heart away from God. Centuries later, the apostle Paul warned Christians against the same thing:

"Don't team up with those who are unbelievers. How can righteousness be a partner with wickedness? How can light live with darkness? What harmony can there be between Christ and the devil? How can a believer be a partner with an unbeliever? And what union can there be between God's temple and idols? For we are the temple of the living God" *(2 Corinthians 6: 14-16).*

Solomon's great sin began with sexual immorality, which is idolatry. What practical use could a man have with a total of 1,000 wives? It is extravagance, which is also idolatry. As Solomon fell deeper and deeper into the enchanted mist of sexual immorality, he drifted farther and farther from the God of his father, David.

"In Solomon's old age, they turned his heart to worship other gods instead of being completely faithful to the Lord his God, as his father, David, had been'" *(1 Kings 11: 4).*

We must never lose sight of the fact that David, in spite of his many sins, is considered faithful to the Lord. The difference between David and Solomon is in their hearts. David's heart was never turned away from the Lord as Solomon's was.

"Solomon worshiped Ashtoreth, the goddess of the Sidonians **(one of many fertility goddesses of ancient times associated with Baal. Eventually these goddesses morphed into Aphrodite, the goddess of love to the Greeks),** *and Molech, the detestable god of the Ammonites* **(Israelites sacrificed children to Molech. Christians today consider abortion the modern equivalent to the worship of Molech).** *In this way, Solomon did what was evil in the Lord's sight; he refused to follow the Lord completely, as his father, David, had done"* *(1 Kings 11: 4-6).*

15

Paul warns Christians against sexual immorality, which is idolatry. He also explains the effect of sexual immorality on a person's body, which is the new temple of God:

"Run from sexual sin! <u>No other sin so clearly affects the body as this one does. For sexual immorality is a sin against your own body.</u> Don't you realize that your body is the temple of the Holy Spirit, who lives in you and was given to you by God?" (1 Corinthians 6: 18, 19).

So the revelation of Jonathan's dream began to take shape in his consciousness. And Raphael continued to wait, expectantly. The Healing Angel gazed upon the splendor of God's throne and waited for his next instruction. Meanwhile, Jonathan continued to read.

"On the Mount of Olives, east of Jerusalem, he even built a pagan shrine for Chemosh, the detestable god of Moab, and another for Molech, the detestable god of the Ammonites. Solomon built such shrines for all his foreign wives to use for burning incense and sacrificing to their gods.

*The Lord was very angry with Solomon, **<u>for his heart had turned away from the Lord, the God of Israel, who had appeared to him twice</u>**. He had warned Solomon specifically about worshiping other gods (idolatry), but Solomon dis not listen to the Lord's command" (1 Kings 11: 7-10).*

And Jonathan continued to ruminate on what he was learning. The interpretation of the dream was taking form, beginning to crystalize. He took out his notebook and wrote what he'd learned:

- *Solomon was the son of David. He was the one God specifically chose to build the Temple of the Lord, the dwelling place of God's Holy Spirit on earth. But Solomon disobeyed the Lord. He succumbed to sexual immorality and married women who worshiped other gods, which God had specifically instructed him not to do. Because of his marriages to idolaters, Solomon's heart was turned away from the Lord.*

And here Jonathan had a question. Did Solomon die out of favor with God? Surely not, or he wouldn't be "our first great king." Jonathan was perplexed. He'd heard scholars argue both sides of this point. Jonathan had to discover the truth. And Raphael whispered into his ear...not in audible words, but rather in tiny desires placed upon his charge's heart. The Angel encouraged Jonathan to keep up the pursuit, continue to search God's word. "It's there," the Angel whispered.

So Jonathan kept searching. And he found the answer to his question. The Lord had sent word to David through Nathan, the prophet:

*"When your days are over and you rest with your fathers, I will raise up your offspring to succeed you, **who will come from your own body**, and I will establish his kingdom. He is the one who will build a house for my Name, and I will establish the throne of his kingdom forever. I will be his father, and he will be my son. **When he does wrong**, I will punish him with the rod of men, with floggings inflicted by men. **But my love will never be taken away from him, as I took it away from Saul, whom I removed from before you**"* (2 Samuel 7: 12-15).

It still remained for Jonathan to discover exactly how Solomon was our first great King. And if he was our first great King, and he came after David, who was the next great King and how many great Kings are there?

And then the Healing Angel led the dreamer to Nehemiah. Jonathan learned that Nehemiah served as the cup-bearer for King Artaxerxes. This Persian king had allowed a remnant of Jews to return to their homeland after the Babylonian captivity. Nehemiah received word from the Israelites concerning Jerusalem: "They said to me, 'Things are not going well for those who returned to the province of Judah. They are in great trouble and disgrace. The wall of Jerusalem has been torn down, and the gates have been destroyed by fire" (Nehemiah 1: 3).

Nehemiah mourned and fasted for days, then prayed to the Lord that Artaxerxes would act favorably toward him. And the Lord answered Nehemiah's prayer. King Artaxerxes gave Nehemiah permission to travel to Jerusalem and undertake the task of rebuilding the wall around their city.

In addition to rebuilding the wall, Nehemiah found need to reform the Jews spiritually as well. Their faith had deteriorated significantly and they were not faithful to the God of their ancestors. Even the elders and the priests were engulfed in sin and profaning the Name of the God of Abraham, Isaac, and Jacob. At the end of the Book of Nehemiah, Jonathan began to understand why Solomon was our first great King, and that only two great Kings were needed for God to accomplish his purpose on earth. Nehemiah explained:

*"About the same time I realized that some of the men of Judah **had married women from Ashdod, Ammon, and Moab**. Furthermore, half their children spoke the language of Ashdod or of some other people **and could not speak the language of Judah at all**. So I confronted them and called down curses on them. I beat some of them and pulled out their hair. I made them swear in the name of God that **they would not let their children intermarry with the pagan people of the land.***

***"Wasn't this exactly what led King Solomon of Israel into sin?"** I demanded. "There was no king from any nation who could compare to him, **and God loved him and made him King over all Israel. But even he was led into sin by his foreign wives** (unbelievers). How could you even think of committing this sinful deed and act unfaithfully toward God by marrying foreign women?"* (Nehemiah 13: 23-27).

And Jonathan went back to his notebook, writing down what he was learning:

- *Solomon failed because of excess, because of lust and the idolatry that sexual immorality opened the door to. Solomon was disobedient to the laws and decrees set down by the Lord in the Law of Moses. He disobeyed the very law that was contained in the Ark of the Covenant, which was kept in the Temple Solomon built:*

  "The king must not build up a large stable of horses for himself or send his people to Egypt to buy horses, for the Lord has told you, 'You must never return to Egypt.' **(Solomon made an alliance with Pharaoh by marrying his daughter)**. <u>*The king must not take many wives for himself, because they will turn his heart away from the Lord*</u>*" (Deuteronomy 17: 16, 17).*

  Seven hundred wives and three hundred concubines. The excess is unfathomable. Solomon had become a prisoner to lust.

Jonathan understood that Solomon was the human descendent of David, a man born of human flesh and bone, which caused him to be born in sin. He understood that Solomon built the physical Temple of the Lord, which housed the Law, which was written in stone. He understood that a second son from David's lineage had to come, Jesus, born not of human flesh but of the Holy Spirit. And he understood what Jesus meant when he told the Pharisees, "Destroy this temple (temple of Solomon), and in three days I will raise it up" (John 2: 19).

Solomon, human son of David, built the physical Temple of the Lord which can be destroyed; Jesus, Divine son of David, established the spiritual Temple which lasts forever, and can never be destroyed. Jonathan understood that all who have put their faith in Jesus are now the living temple of the Holy Spirit. So in this sense, Solomon was our first great king (son of David), and Jesus accomplished what Solomon, who lived under the Law, could not; righteousness with God through his blood. Whereas the Law of Moses, which was written in stone and kept in the physical Temple of Solomon, could not make anyone righteous; the New Covenant, sealed by the blood of Jesus, enabled God's Law to be written on the hearts of all those who would believe.

Obviously then, Solomon was our first great King and Jesus *IS* our true and everlasting King, also born from the line of David as far as his humanity is concerned.

So Jonathan mulled it all over in his mind. And Raphael watched, and waited. Jonathan knew – in his knowing place – the journey had only just begun. He was in that turbulent state, where the more he learned the foggier his mind became. He continued to thrash and flail to and fro.

And one day something happened that threw him deeper into the whirlwind, farther into the mystery. A minister prophesied over the troubled lad: *"You have the spirit of Elijah upon you. And the spirit of Jezebel is pursuing you. Be courageous and finish the race that has been marked out for you."*

Jonathan pleaded with the minister to explain the meaning of this word, but the minister could not. "The word is for you. Only you can know the meaning in the end. It is God's word to you, it was not meant for me." Tears welled up in Jonathan's eyes. He was suspended between the Holy Word of God and the profane life he was living. "I wish you good fortune, my friend," the minister said. "This much I can say for sure...you must learn how to defeat the spirit of Jezebel. Honestly, I do not envy you, but God knows what he's doing."

So Jonathan tumbled. And he desperately begged God to help him. And Raphael watched, and waited. And finally the Almighty dispatched the Healing Angel to the young man. Raphael delivered the message to Jonathan as he slept:

"Your first dream from the Lord will remain the base and foundation of all he speaks to you. Every message you receive afterwards will in some way lead you back to the first message. And each time your journey brings you back to the first message, new revelation will unfold. There are many more messages to come, but each in their time and not one twinkling of an eye before. For now, discover John the Baptist and discover how the spirit of Elijah was upon him, and learn why the spirit of Elijah was upon him. And learn about Elijah's adversaries and what they have to do with your present time.

You have always been a dreamer. You have always imagined yourself a real-life knight in shining armor. You will have your opportunity to be a true knight, a true hero, but you have no idea at present what a knight in the service of the Lord is about. The Almighty will illuminate your understanding through that which you best understand. The world of knights and quests makes sense to you and the Lord will teach you through these tales. Be careful and be diligent: bring every thought to the obedience of Christ. If you come across something that stirs your spirit, test it against the Word of God. And learn the ways of the Holy Spirit. And understand that the Holy Spirit is God; he is not a servant to be ordered here and there by humans. You live in the time of the Holy Spirit's ministry on earth and he is Lord.

Prepare for a long, arduous journey. Continue on your quest for the Holy Grail, but know that the true Grail is not an object; it is not a thing to be achieved. The true Grail, you dreamy-eyed knight, is a state of being; this state of being begins with learning true compassion and finds its peace in the knowledge and experience of Grace.

I am Raphael. I sit in the presence of the Lord Almighty. Learn my purpose and be faithful to the Lord Jesus Christ, for it is through him and by him I was created. I have delivered the entire message that was entrusted to me. Holy, holy is the Lord. To him be all honor and glory forever, amen.

***

"Where do I begin?" Jonathan felt as though a drain was inside his skull, and his brain was swirling downward. Solomon, the Grail, Elijah, Jezebel, John the Baptist. Where to begin?

Jonathan's life took him down many roads; he encountered brief visits to the peak of the mountain and long seasons in the valley of despair. He muddled through life, sometimes with the purpose of a juggernaut, and sometimes he meandered with lack of direction. But always he imagined himself a true knight in shining armor. And he wandered and he wondered; and he sojourned and then strayed off the intended path many times. Sometimes he medicated the pain and sometimes he followed the desires of his heart toward the Light. Sometimes he felt holy, but most of the time his depravity sickened him. But he never forgot the dreams and he never doubted that God had spoken to him. And one day it happened. Reading his Bible, with no particular purpose in mind, the Holy Spirit illuminated Jonathan's knowing place from within. The words seemed to elevate themselves from the page:

*"He will be a man with the spirit and power of Elijah. He will prepare the people for the coming of the Lord. **He will turn the hearts of the fathers to their children**, and he will cause those who are rebellious to accept the wisdom of the godly" (Luke 1: 17).*

And Jonathan's spirit stirred within. Immediately, he recalled the word of prophecy spoken over him by the minister twenty-five years earlier. And Jonathan came one step closer to his purpose on earth. Jonathan pondered the incident whence Gabriel came to the priest Zechariah, John the Baptist's father. Gabriel told Zechariah the son in his wife's womb would have the

22

spirit of Elijah upon him, and that his son would "turn the hearts of the fathers to their children." And Jonathan remembered Raphael as he read aloud, but to himself: *"Then the angel said, 'I am Gabriel! I stand in the very presence of God. It was he who sent me to bring you this good news!'"* *(Luke 1: 19).*

Jonathan shivered as he recalled the night Raphael visited him while he slept. And Raphael looked at Gabriel. The two angels gazed at each other, in wonderment. Then both of them turned to gaze upon the brightness indescribable. And both of the angels watched, and waited.

And Jonathan recalled the message delivered by Raphael all those years ago. He recalled that he must discover why John the Baptist had the spirit of Elijah upon him. He must also discover who Elijah was and who his adversaries were. He must also pursue the true Grail and find out what Solomon had to do with it. And then he found Ahab:

*"Ahab son of Omri began to rule over Israel in the thirty-eighth year of King Asa's reign in Judah. He reigned in Samaria twenty-two years. **But Ahab son of Omri did what was evil in the Lord's sight, even more than any of the kings before him. And as though it were not enough to follow the sinful example of Jeroboam, he married Jezebel, the daughter of king Ethbaal of the Sidonians, and he began to bow down in worship of Baal**"* *(1 Kings 16: 29-31).*

Ahab did more evil in the Lord's eyes than any of the kings before him, which included marrying Jezebel of the Sidonians, who caused him to bow down in worship of Baal. Jonathan remembered the minister who prophesied that the spirit of Jezebel was against him. This meant that it is not a particular woman, but rather a spirit that had attached itself to her, and thus, since then has been associated with the particular woman's name. Further proof of this is found in the Book of Revelation, as Jesus is addressing the Christian church of Thyatira, centuries after the woman Jezebel had died. The same way in which John the Baptist was not himself Elijah, but had the spirit of Elijah upon him.

"Write this letter to the angel of the church in Thyatira. This is the message from the Son of God, whose eyes are like flames of fire, whose feet are like polished bronze:

"I know all the things you do. I have seen your love, your faith, your service, and your patient endurance...

"**But I have this complaint against you. You are permitting that woman – that Jezebel who calls herself a prophet – to lead my servants astray** (one of her goals is to destroy men of God)**. She teaches them to commit sexual sin and to eat food offered to idols** (her most effective tool is sexual immorality).

"I gave her time to repent, but she does not want to turn away from her immorality (She will not acknowledge authority).

"Therefore, I will throw her on a bed of suffering, **and those who commit adultery with her will suffer greatly unless they repent and turn away from her evil deeds**" (Revelation 2: 18-22).

As Jonathan meditated on the words of Jesus, he was reminded of Solomon once again. With the knowledge that it was not a particular woman, but a spirit named after a particular woman, Jonathan began to understand Solomon's downfall on a deeper level. Was it, perhaps, this same spirit that caused Solomon to fall under the spell of lust and sexual immorality? A man with one thousand wives is in bondage; he is in the grips of something more powerful than himself. While meditating on this, Jonathan was led to the words of Solomon himself:

While I was at the window of my house, looking through the curtain, I saw some naïve young men, **and one in particular who lacked common sense**. He was crossing the street near the house of an immoral woman, strolling down the path by her house. It was twilight, in the evening, as deep darkness fell. The woman approached him, seductively dressed and sly of heart. She was the brash, rebellious type, never content to stay at home. She is often in the streets and *markets, soliciting at every corner.* __**She threw her arms around him**__ __**and kissed him**__*, and with a brazen look she said, "I've just made my peace offerings and fulfilled my vows.* __**You are the one I was looking**__ __**for! I came out to find you and here you are!**__ *My bed is spread with beautiful blankets, with colored sheets of Egyptian linen. I've perfumed my bed with myrrh, aloes, and cinnamon. Come, let's drink our fill of love until morning. Let's enjoy each other's caresses, for my husband is not home. He's away on a long trip. He has taken a wallet full of money with him and won't return until later this month.*

So she seduced him with her pretty speech and enticed him with her flattery. __**He followed her at once, like an ox going to the**__ __**slaughter**__*. He was like a stag caught in a trap, awaiting the arrow that would pierce its heart. He was like a bird flying into a snare,* __**little**__ __**knowing it would cost him his life**__*.*

So listen to me, my sons, and pay attention to my words. Don't let your hearts stray away toward her. Don't wander down her wayward path. __**For she has been the ruin of many; many men have been**__ __**her victims. Her house is the road to the grave. Her bedroom is**__ __**the den of death**__ *(Proverbs 7: 6-27).*

The woman being described by Solomon is the personification of what has come to be known as the Jezebel spirit. Ahab might have been the worst, but he was not the first. Solomon had fallen victim to the same evil spirit, because of his marriages to foreign women (unbelievers), and his subsequent bowing down to their gods. Remembering his encouragement from Raphael, Jonathan set out to learning about Elijah's adversaries, beginning with Jezebel, who was under the control of an evil spirit. Jonathan went to his notebook and recorded what he'd learned:

- ***Jezebel was the daughter of a Sidonian king*** (Sidonians are included in the nations God had instructed the Israelites not to marry)**, *and a worshiper of Baal. The worship of Baal***

incorporated both animal and child sacrifices, ritualistic sensual dancing, and sodomy by male and female Baal prostitutes.

- **Jezebel came from a background and an environment where sex acts, sodomy and every form of sensual and licentious living was exalted as being a way to tap into the power of the false gods they worshiped.** (Jezebel's spirit runs rampant in the pornographic industry today, which is so easily accessible to teens).

- **To accomplish her goal of instituting idolatry among God's people, Jezebel kill's God's prophets:** "Once when Jezebel had tried to kill all the Lord's prophets, Obadiah had hidden 100 of them in two caves. He put fifty prophets in each cave and supplied them with food and water" (1 Kings 18: 4).

- **Jezebel spawns and supports false prophets:** "Elijah replied (to Ahab), 'You and your family are the troublemakers, for you have refused to obey the commands of the Lord and have worshiped the images of Baal instead. Now summon all Israel to join me at Mount Carmel, along with the 450 prophets of Baal and the 400 prophets of Asherah who are supported by Jezebel" (1 Kings 18: 18, 19).

- 1 Kings 21: 8-11 – "So she wrote letters in Ahab's name, sealed them with his seal, and sent them to the elders and other leaders of the town where Naboth lived. In her letters she commanded: 'Call the citizens together for a time of fasting, and give Naboth a place of honor. And then seat two scoundrels across from him who will accuse him of cursing God and the king. Then take him out and stone him to death.'" **–Jezebel lies and assumes a legitimate leader's authority for herself. Notice the anonymity involved in this deception. Jezebel is not prominent, everyone thought the king had issued the orders. Notice Jezebel's** *expertise in utilizing "religion" to achieve her ends, "Call the citizens together for a time of fasting..."*

- *Jezebel is an arrogantly and proudly self-appointed "prophetess." She establishes herself as a teacher of God's people and misleads them into sexual immorality:* "But I have this complaint against you. You are permitting that woman — that Jezebel who calls herself a prophet — to lead my servants astray. She teaches them to commit sexual sin and to eat food offered to idols" (Revelation 2: 20).

- *Jezebel is stubborn, unrepentant, proud and arrogant, unwilling to repent of her ungodly behavior and ungodly influence on the people of God.*

- *Jezebel uses sexual immorality, sodomy, and every form of sensual and licentious living to gain power and control. This flesh factor is utilized to gain its own purposes.*

- *To accomplish the goal of instituting sexual licentiousness, sensuality, idolatry, and witchcraft among God's people, Jezebel today (spiritually) kills God's true prophets. This spirit will make every effort to accuse, slander, and otherwise verbally attack the true prophet of God. Sexual lusts are a tool which Jezebel uses to achieve its goal of total control.*

- *Jezebel will relentlessly utilize sexuality, sensuality, idolatry, witchcraft and every devious and demonic means to come against the true prophet of God.*

- *This spirit knows how to make itself attractive and how to charm and seduce a righteous person right out of their virtue.*[3]

Jonathan realized that both Ahab, and Solomon before him, relinquished spiritual authority to the gods of their foreign wives. Not only in their homes, but in the entire kingdom. At this moment of understanding, Raphael was dispatched to earth. The Healing Angel led the questing knight toward the true Grail. The angel whispered into the man's knowing place: "Find the true Grail."

So Jonathan set out to find the true Grail. Unbeknownst to himself, he made all the same mistakes others have made through the centuries on their quest for the truth of the matter. Jonathan made progress in stages – accompanied by failures – and after twenty-seven years of trial and tribulation – and two moments where he stood on the precipice of the suicidal abyss, truly yearning for death the same way Elijah had once done when being threatened by Jezebel – the blurred images and lessons clouded in mist crystalized as Raphael visited him for the second time in his sleep. The discourse of Raphael to Jonathan:

God has put it in your heart to become a godly husband and father. Remember the prayer you uttered at the age of fifteen? You said, "God, please make me the best husband and father in the world." You've come to believe, over the next forty years, that God's answer to your prayer was 'NO.' What you didn't know then, at the tender age of fifteen, is that what you asked of God was no small thing. As a matter of fact, your request would have taken many years to accomplish even for a young man born into a healthy, God-fearing family. Because you were born into a family of spiritual and emotional brokenness, a family full of abuse in many forms, forty years was necessary. And only now that you have finally come to the point where you have relinquished even your heart's greatest desire – to be a husband and father – are you able to fulfill the purpose God set for you since before the world began.

You have been in search of the true Grail. Now that you have been completely stripped of your narcissism, and self-absorption, and self-serving motives, you are finally ready to achieve the Grail. Remember the lines of poetry you stumbled across twenty-four years ago? It was the

Holy Spirit who led you to those inspired words. You weren't able to accept it then, but the words applied to your plight:

When God wants to drill a man,
And thrill a man,
And skill a man,
When God wants to mold a man to play the noblest part;
When he yearns with all his heart to create so great and bold a man
That all the world shall be amazed,
Watch his methods, watch his ways!
How he ruthlessly perfects
Whom he royally elects!
How he hammers and hurts him,
And with mighty blows converts him
Into trial shapes of clay which only God understands;
While his tortured heart is crying and he lifts up beseeching hands!
How he uses whom he chooses,
And with every purpose fuses him;
By every act induces him to try his splendor out –
God knows what he's about.

- anonymous

The true Grail is not an object to be grasped, but rather, it is a state of being. The foundation of the Grail is **Compassion.** *Remember your first dream? You were given a test. God's testing, from Abraham to Job, is done for one purpose, that is, to bring the person closer to the image of Christ. The true hero must first learn what compassion is. One must have a gentle heart; a heart capable of love, not simply of lust. The word* **Compassion** *means "Suffering With."* **Passion** *is "suffering," and* **Com** *is "with." The true man of God must suffer things for love and prove that he is not ruled by lust.*

King David's human son, Solomon, inherited the throne of God's kingdom on earth. God's kingdom, under Solomon's rule, became a spiritual wasteland. The whole kingdom suffered because the King surrendered his spiritual authority for the temporal and fleeting pleasures of lust. Solomon lived under the Law, which brings death. The Word made flesh, God's only begotten Son, born of the lineage of King David as far as his humanity is concerned, came to the world to restore the wasteland. The sacrifice of Jesus on The Cross saved humanity from the consequences of sin under the Law. Jesus accomplished in his body what the Law, housed in the Temple Solomon built, could not – freedom from the spiritual death that sin brings. Jesus will return to earth again, to establish his kingdom forever. Since his ascension into heaven where he sits at the right hand of The Almighty Creator, his kingdom on earth has, by stages, deteriorated into a wasteland once again.

Just as John the Baptist had the spirit of Elijah upon him and came to prepare the way for the Lord's first appearance on earth, the kingdom is in need of servants again with the spirit of Elijah to prepare the way for the final coming of the Lord Jesus Christ. When he comes again, he will refresh the wasteland once for all and his kingdom will have no end.

Your propensity toward magical kingdoms, where gallant knights fight for justice and win the hand of the princess, was, in the beginning, a defense mechanism born out of necessity. Your life was so filled with pain, abuse, and brokenness, you sought refuge in the magical kingdom, where justice prevails and where impossible situations are overcome by a knight with purity of heart. But eventually the real world must be addressed. Fortunately for you, The Almighty has a plan for you where the real world parallels what humans consider legend. Your quest is for a treasure that restores the spiritual wasteland which truly exists.

The true quest is a young man's spiritual development from the foolishness of puberty to the full consciousness of manliness with its accompanying masculine obligations of husband and father. Your earthly father was absent. Your earthly mother was unable to give the love you needed because of her own brokenness. As a result, you were left to your own devices. You sought love and affirmation in the arms of the first girl you found romance with. Because she fulfilled your need for love, and eased the pain when you embraced her, you believed she was the princess.

In the legend, through humiliation, blunders, discomforts, and hardships the knight wins his way, loses it again and again, until he finally understands the responsibilities of marriage, kingship, and the high priesthood. Remember the day your princess informed you she was pregnant? You were seventeen years old, she was a year younger. You set your heart on marrying her, but her father, an unbeliever, stole her away one night while you slept, drove three hours east and paid the clinic three hundred dollars to end your son's life. I thought The Almighty would dispatch me to your side that night, but he never gave the order. Instead, Jesus presented a supplication to his Father and the Holy Spirit brought you the gift of sleep. The Almighty instructed me to keep watch over you from that night forward because your service on earth would require a man forged in the fire of pain inexpressible. Many times since that night I thought you would give up, and many times you wanted to, but God's Holy Spirit moved you along – always gave you the courage to continue, even if it was only for one more day.

*To achieve the true Grail, you had to learn **Grace**. When you naively set out on your quest all those years ago, you were so weak and wanting in faith that you believed you could achieve more by your own prowess than by the Grace of our Lord. As long as you believed it was by your own deeds you would attain the goal, dishonor lied in wait for you and your hopes would come to nothing. But the Holy Spirit held out a promise to you that you never let go of, and that promise was in the form of a dream that set the course of your life. You need only to persevere so that when you have done the will of God, you will receive what he has promised.*

You have been granted experiential truth into what philosophers and psychological scientists have sought after for centuries. You have one advantage the philosophers and scientists did not. Through the Holy Spirit of God, you have been given the ability to see the truth behind the stories. You've been given an insight into the language of God that His prophets possess, but scientists without the Holy Spirit continue to fall short of. The psychologist Carl Jung knocked on the door of Truth, but he never entered into that Truth because he lacked dependence on God's

Spirit. You will be given access to the ultimate truth behind the door Jung was knocking on. He came to the conclusion that "Myths are not mere words or stories but living truths and psychic realities that exercise their power on the human soul by their use of Symbolic Language. Symbols thus serve as the vehicles of psychic transformation that extend beyond the communication of meaning to the level of psychic integration and spiritual revitalization…The propositions in the Bible are in effect psychic facts and relevant to psychic truths that are concerned with the illumination of the soul."[4] You will find the ultimate truth about God's language Jung could not, because you have been born of the Spirit.

The Creator will continue to speak to you in dreams, through parables and symbols. You must always bring the symbols to the obedience of Christ and test them against the Word of God. If you remain diligent in this matter, you will come to know experientially what our Lord spoke to Nicodemus: "No one can enter the kingdom of God unless he is born of water and the Spirit. Flesh gives birth to flesh, but the Spirit gives birth to spirit."[5] And also what Jesus spoke to the Samaritan woman at the well: "Yet a time is coming and has now come when the true worshipers will worship the Father in spirit and truth, for they are the kind of worshipers the Father seeks. God is spirit, and his worshipers must worship in spirit and in truth."[6] And you must never let go of these words spoken by The Savior: "But when he, the Spirit of truth, comes, he will guide you into all truth. He will not speak on his own; he will speak only what he hears, and he will tell you what is yet to come. He will bring glory to me by taking from what is mine and making it known to you."[7] And, finally, hold the prayer Jesus prayed to The Father close to your heart: "Sanctify them by the truth; your word is truth."[8]

In the legend of the Grail, the maimed Fisher King's realm has become mysteriously barren and waste. The King has been maimed between his thighs which has left him impotent. A maimed King is not fit to rule and his infirmity has rendered the land desolate. The King had fallen in love with a beautiful woman outside the Grail line, which is the same mistake Solomon made when he married Pharaoh's daughter and made an alliance with Egypt. In the legend, the King had ridden from the castle with the cry, "Amours" on his lips and promptly met a pagan knight from the holy lands. They fought and the pagan knight was killed, but in the battle the King had been wounded between the thighs by the poisonous tip of a lance which had broken off. When it was withdrawn from the wound there was an inscription which read "Grail."

The pagan knight, born in Paradise, wounded the King with a lance. The King could not be healed, but the Grail kept him alive, which was an exquisite torture to the poor man. He became known as the "Fisher King" because each night his subjects would place him in a boat where he would sit and fish. It was his only pleasure. The fish is the Christian symbol of Jesus. Only one thing can bring about the healing of the King, and that is a knight who will ask the question: "What ails you, uncle?" The question is proof the knight has learned Compassion.

The lance, or spear, or sword, is that which both heals and wounds. It offers insight yet wounds that which is corrupt. The spear renders impotent whosoever it strikes, leaving him in a strange state in which he can neither be healed nor actually die. This lays waste his lands and only a hero of exceptional powers and worthiness is able to lift the burden and heal the sufferer by using the selfsame spear that wounded him. And this, beautiful dreamer, is where your genius lies; the very same place in which you have been wounded. The land is waste today because of absent fathers who have not been trained in matters of the Grail.

There is a legendary sword of King David, which Solomon's wife placed in the ship of Solomon to be sent down the ages until the Grail Knights discover it. Solomon's wife placed the weapon in a ship she had built, which sailed out into the ages and was finally discovered by three Christian Knights – Galahad, Perceval, and Bors. When they found the wondrous sword, Perceval's sister Dindraine, tells them of its history. It was the unsheathing by unworthy hands that caused the wasteland, which the hero must now restore. The last hand which used the sword, before they found it, was that of the Fisher King who was wounded between the thighs and made impotent by a lance. According to this selfsame legend, Lancelot and Galahad and Perceval are descended from the royal line of David and Solomon.[9] And now call to mind the words of Jesus, the First and the Last King, born of the line of David as far as his humanity is concerned, the King of Kings said to his disciples: "Do not suppose that I have come to bring peace to the earth. I did not come to bring peace, but a sword" (Matthew 10: 34).

Jonathan, your heart's strongest desire has always been to become a husband and father, but you never learned what a godly husband and father is entrusted with. You are the Fisher King who rode out with the cry of "Amours" on your lips. But you were unworthy of kingship and priesthood, which is what the true Grail demands. When you fell in love at the age of seventeen, you were still made of base metal, you had not yet been refined into gold. Your heart was filled with lust, which caused your princess to become pregnant out of wedlock. Your son's life was taken, just as David's son was taken because of his adulterous affair with Bathsheba. And you have followed in the ways of David's son Solomon, who lost sight of the Grail as a result of the downward spiral brought about through uncontrollable lust. You live in a wasteland full of boys being born out of wedlock who never learn what it means to be a godly man. You have been disciplined by God very severely, just as David was. The time has come for you to accept that discipline and consider it a gift instead of a curse. God disciplines those he accepts as sons. The time has come for you to accept God's discipline with joy instead of with weeping and self-pity. Stand up, man! Self-pity is what Jezebel uses to control her victims! Are you to play the role of victim all your life? When you were young, you knew no better. But the time has come for you to let go of the past and be a man. Be strong and courageous of heart. The Lord has not left you orphaned.

According to the legend, three Christian Knights find Solomon's ship – Galahad, Perceval, and Bors. Western Civilization has taken Galahad and mad him the Grail Knight and through the ages the Grail became the cup Jesus drank from at the Last Supper. Western Civilization has adopted a tale wherein Joseph of Arimathea takes this cup to England where a castle resembling King Solomon's temple is built to hold the Grail. Since that time, Knights who are sworn to celibacy guard the Grail. Your quest, however, and your life, is to find the true Grail, which is the truth that lies behind the stories. You must learn who Perceval was and in the process realize that which is true. It is time for your life to become real. It is time for you to step out of the enchanted mist and into the sphere of God's truth and bring a new reality to the spiritual wasteland on earth.

Remember your first dream? Remember your response to the question, "Who was Solomon?" You answered that he was our first great King. And the teacher, who is wisdom born of the fear of the Lord, replied, "I'll accept that answer,"

The legendary ship that Solomon's wife built, the ship containing the sword of David which has the power to heal the wounded Fisher King, consider the ship. Solomon's wife says to him, "Sire, I have thought how a knight will be descended from our lineage." [10] That knight is Perceval, and your quest is similar to the Perceval who was lost long ago, buried under the hubris of the Galahad of Arthurian legend. But The Almighty has chosen to speak to you through legend, because that is what you understand. Heed this warning, though: you must never fail to bring every thought to the obedience of Christ. Whatever stirs your spirit, you must test against the Word of God. The ship of Solomon represents Christ. Just as the ship carries a man across the sea without peril, upholding him over water, so Christ carries servants through the world and through sins which do not contaminate them. It is your faith in Christ which enables you to be blameless in the presence of God.

In the legend, Perceval is aided by Gawain, the knight with the highest integrity, who represents Perceval's heart. Gawain counsels Perceval to beware of sin which he seems to prefer to affliction. [11] He also helps Perceval understand that it is himself he must conquer. Jonathan, your life and your calling is the personification of the truth behind Perceval. The symbol of the Grail is the ox, which represents patience under suffering and you have suffered much, but much of your suffering has been brought on by yourself. Just as the ox is stubborn, and will beat its head against the rails repeatedly, you have been slow to accept correction in certain areas.

A young person is allowed by God freely to choose between ignorance and learning, between purity and corruption. Perceval, like yourself, during his initiations, which become more arduous as he advances in power over himself and his environment, dreams vividly and recalls each dream after awakening. Perceval, though it has taken him so long, has learned humility and now it is time for him to fight his last battle, that with his brother, Feirefiz.

The battle is a reenacting of the ill-fated fight between the Fisher King and the pagan knight who wounded him so terribly. But this time the outcome will be completely different. The battle is the most difficult either has ever fought. Feirefiz is protected by armor which draws its power from the sub-earthly will, whereas Perceval draws strength from the super-earthly for he has conquered doubt in God. Thus, the three-fold nature of man is revealed in Perceval as the head, Gawain the heart, and Feirefiz as the loins and will of sinful nature.

Perceval is loyal and steadfast; Feirefiz ruled by sinful nature; Gawain is the healing force of love. Feirefiz finally says to Perceval: "To strive with myself have I ridden, and went near myself to slay, thy valor in good stead has stood us, from myself has thou saved me today." Feeling entirely at one with another, as if something essential had been missing before, they are welcomed by Gawain at the Castle of Marvels. Amidst the celebrations, however, because he has learned humility, Perceval takes Feirefiz to the Grail Castle, that he might heal the King. He has been instructed since the beginning of his quest, to be alert and ask the right question. By now it is not the question itself which is important but it is the questioning that heals. It is in the question that Perceval shows he has learned Compassion.

Perceval finally arrives at the Grail Castle where all awaited him sadly; for he had taken such a long time to find it. And angels in heaven are awaiting you in sadness, Jonathan. Forty years is long enough.

When Perceval enters the room where the Fisher King lays, the King asks Perceval to let him die, which meant, to permit him not to have to look upon the Grail for seven nights and eight days. That would suffice to let death take its course. Remember the night you asked God to let you die, Jonathan. Take heed, you have been forgiven that, just as Elijah was forgiven when he asked God to let him die. Self-pity is a sin, but not unforgivable, move on. When Elijah begged the Lord to let him die, the Lord told him, "Get up and eat, for the journey ahead of you is long." [12] *And I say the same to you now.*

Upon hearing the Fisher King's request, Perceval wept and prayed on his knees that the King be released from his agony. He asked him: "What ails you, uncle?" At once, the Fisher King's face relaxed into softness, for he had been released by Christ who brought Lazarus back from the dead. The Fisher King came forth beautiful again, all pain removed. All glory and honor to the Lord, Jesus Christ.

And now you shall understand the true Grail. It is found in denying the self, indeed, allowing yourself to be crucified with Christ. It is found in the re-birth and transformation of the individual, giving rise to love and compassion. And be careful to understand this, Jonathan, the Grail is found only when Faith replaces the need to perform works. The long awaited Grail Knight performed Divine acts because he bathed in the Grace of God. God's secrets, like the Grail, are accessible to mankind only through Grace.

Grace is the meaning of the Grail.

You live in a spiritual wasteland which needs to be restored before the Lord returns for the final time. You have learned much about how Solomon failed, which brought the wasteland before the Lord's first coming. There is more to be learned: go farther. You must also learn why Elijah's spirit must come again to prepare the way for the Lord. Learn the ways of the evil spirit known as "Jezebel" for that spirit has wreaked havoc since the beginning of man's time on earth. Discover the ways of the demon called Asmodeus and learn my purpose. I am Raphael and I sit in the presence of God Almighty. Come, Elijah. All glory and honor to the Lord, Jesus Christ, forever, amen.

***

The same spirit that influenced Ahab's wife, Jezebel, has wreaked havoc since the beginning of man's time on earth? Discover the ways of the demon called Asmodeus? Learn Raphael's purpose? Not knowing where else to begin, Jonathan went to the Garden of Eden.

Jonathan learned that according to the Hebrews, Asmodeus is the son of Naamah and Shamdon. He was part of the seraphim, the highest order of angels, but fell from grace when Lucifer was cast from heaven. Jonathan also found a Hebrew legend in which Asmodeus is associated with Lilith, the demon queen of lust. Asmodeus is a fallen angel who became the demon of lechery. His primary goal is to wreck new marriages and force husbands to commit adultery.

Asmodeus was one of the infernal agents blamed for the obscene sexual possession of the Louviers nuns in 17th century France, during the height of the witch scare that ran through Europe. The incident occurred at a convent in Louviers in 1647, and involved eighteen nuns who allegedly were possessed through the bewitchments of the nunnery's director and the vicar of Louviers. According to the confessions – most exacted under torture – the possessed nuns committed unspeakable sexual acts with the Devil and demons; attended witches Sabbaths where they ate babies; and uttered obscenities and spoke in tongues. The nuns were subject to public exorcisms. The vicar, Father Thomas Boulle, was burned alive. The body of the nunnery director, Mathurin Picard, who died before sentencing was passed, was exhumed and burned. A nun who leaked the story to authorities, Sister Madeleine Bavent, was sentenced to the dungeon.[13]

At this point in his research, Jonathan began to question the validity of his message from Raphael. Nuns eating babies? Those same nuns committing sexual acts with the Devil? This is clearly the stuff of superstition. The next day, however, Jonathan stumbled across Lilith.

He began his day reading from the gospel of Matthew. And once again, a passage seemed to be elevated from the rest of the text:

"Jesus called his twelve disciples to him and gave them authority to drive out impure spirits and to heal every disease and sickness" *(Matthew 10: 1).*

Not sure what to do with this verse, and not at all sure if it was the Holy Spirit who had brought the verse to his attention, Jonathan continued his research. According to Hebrew mythology, Adam had slept with the demoness, Lilith, and another like her named Naamah (the supposed mother of Asmodeus). From these demons sprang innumerable demons that still plague mankind. Many generations later, Lilith and Naamah came to Solomon's judgment seat, disguised as harlots of Jerusalem. Jonathan immediately went to his Bible and read the account of the two harlots before Solomon in 1 Kings 3: 16-28.

"Some time later two prostitutes came to the king to have an argument settled. 'Please, my lord," one of them began, 'this woman and I live in the same house. I gave birth to a baby while she was with me in the house. Three days later this woman also had a baby. We were alone; there were only two of us in the house.

'But her baby died during the night when she rolled over on it. Then she got up in the night and took my son from beside me while I was asleep. She laid her dead child in my arms and took mine to sleep beside her. And in the morning when I tried to nurse my son, he was dead! But when I looked more closely in the morning light, I saw that it wasn't my son at all.'

Then the other woman interrupted, 'It certainly was your son, and the living child is mine...Then the king said, 'Let's get the facts straight. Both of you claim the living child is yours, and each one says that the dead one belongs to the other. All right, bring me a sword.' So a sword was brought to the king.

Then he said, 'Cut the living child in two, and give half to one woman and half to the other!'

Then the woman who was the real mother of the living child, and who loved him very much, cried out, 'Oh no, my lord! Give her the child – please do not kill him!'

But the other woman said, 'All right, he will be neither yours nor mine; divide him between us!'" (1 Kings 3: 16-26).

Jonathan was apprehensive at the very least. And Raphael gazed on The Almighty. He watched, and waited. Just then, the Holy Spirit illuminated Jonathan's knowing place; the place he was becoming more and more familiar with. And not only more familiar, but more comfortable with as well. Jonathan, being nudged by the Holy Spirit went back to the gospel of Matthew.

"Then they brought him a demon-possessed man who was blind and mute, and Jesus healed him, so that he could both talk and see. All the people were astonished and said, 'Could this be the Son of David?'" (Matthew 12: 22, 23).

And Jonathan, illuminated in his knowing place, meditated. And Raphael watched, and waited. And Jonathan remembered that he was to bring all thoughts to the obedience of Christ. And it occurred to him that whether or not the Hebrew myth about Lilith was entirely true is not the issue. The issue, in fact, is this: is it not entirely possible that the prostitute who took the living child, and then was willing to have that child cut in half, was under the influence of an impure spirit? So Jonathan continued his research.

The Hebrew myth about Lilith recounts a scene where Adam complains to God because Lilith has left him. God at once sends

the angels Senoy, Sansenoy and Semangelof to fetch Lilith back. They found her beside the Red Sea, a region abounding in lascivious demons, to whom she bore *Lilim* at the rate of more than one hundred a day. "Return to Adam without delay," the angels said, "or we will drown you!" Lilith asked: "How can I return to Adam and live like an honest housewife, after my stay beside the Red Sea?" "It will be death to refuse!" they answered. "How can I die," Lilith asked again, "when God has ordered me *to take charge of all newborn children: boys up to the eighth day of life, that of circumcision; girls up to the twentieth day.* Nonetheless, if ever I see your three names or likenesses displayed in an amulet above a newborn child, I promise to spare it." To this they agreed; but God punished Lilith by making one hundred of her demon children perish daily; *and if she could not destroy a human infant, because of the angelic amulet,* she would spitefully turn against her own.[14]

Some say that Lilith ruled as queen in Zmargad, and again in Sheba; and was the demoness who destroyed Job's sons. Yet she escaped the curse of death which overtook Adam, since they had parted long before the Fall. Lilith and Naamah not only strangle infants but also seduce dreaming men, any one of whom, sleeping alone, may become their victim.[15]

Again, Jonathan wondered how any of this could help him. He thought on it and recalled Jezebel in the Bible. She came from a place where child sacrifice to Baal was practiced. After becoming Ahab's wife, Jezebel instituted Baal worship nationwide. Jeremiah recounts an episode where he finds Israelites sacrificing children: *"They have built pagan shrines to Baal in the valley of Ben-Hinnom, and there they sacrifice their sons and daughters to Molech"* (Jeremiah 32: 35). But what does this have to do with America today? We don't sacrifice babies. "Really?" he heard from his knowing place. "We don't sacrifice children?" And then Jonathan felt that dead spot somewhere behind his stomach. "What about your son?" He didn't want to think about it. "She had your son aborted," the knowing place whispered.

Even though the dead spot somewhere behind his stomach became larger, he considered the issue. The spirit which had Jezebel under its influence existed long before Jezebel and still exists today. And it is that spirit which Elijah defeated. If one doesn't focus on the specifics of the Hebrew myth, but on the truth behind the myth, one realizes the "Jezebel Spirit" is not restricted to a certain person or even a certain time period. Then Jonathan recalled the offspring of Lilith and the demons by the Red Sea. They were called *Lilim*. Then Jonathan immediately recalled the flood in the sixth chapter of Genesis. It was the *Nephilim* who were responsible for the decadence that brought the flood. He would examine *The Nephilim* of the Bible when he had finished examining the Hebrew myth.

"Lilith" is derived from the Babylonian-Assyrian word "lilitu," a female demon, or wind spirit – one of a triad mentioned in Babylonian spells. But she appears earlier as "Lillake" on a 2,000 BC Sumerian tablet from Ur containing the tale of Gilgamesh and the Willow Tree. Popular Hebrew etymology seems to have derived "Lilith" from layil, "night"; and she therefore often appears as a hairy night-monster, as she also does in Arabian folklore. Solomon suspected the Queen of Sheba of being Lilith, because she had hairy legs.[16] According to Isaiah 34: 14, 15, Lilith dwells among the desolate ruins of the Edomite Desert where "satyrs," reems, pelicans, jackals, snakes and kites keep her company: *"Desert animals will mingle there with hyenas, their howls filling the night. Wild goats will bleat at one another among the ruins, and Lilith will come there to rest."*

As Jonathan grew tired of examining Lilith in Hebrew myth, and he was on the verge of moving on, he was led to Christian practices concerning the demoness, which, for some reason, he'd not considered before. He discovered that as late as the eighteenth century, it was common practice in many countries to protect new mothers and infants with amulets against Lilith. These amulets still contained the names of the three angels from centuries before. It was believed that if a child laughed in its sleep, it was a sign that Lilith was present. Tapping the child on the nose made the demon go away.[17]

And then, in the last paragraph on the page from the book he was reading, the paragraph he had predetermined would be the last he would read on the subject, he saw the names Elijah and Raphael. The paragraph read as follows:

"Lilith also could be repelled by the saying of any of her numberless names. The basis for this comes from the story (probably Christian Byzantine in origin) about how the prophet Elijah confronted her as she was en route to attack a woman's newborn son, and "to give her the sleep of death, to take her son and drink his blood, to suck the marrow of his bones and to eat his flesh." Elijah forced her to reveal some of her names. Then he excommunicated her.[18]

Lilith probably is related to the Judeo-Hellenistic demon Obizoth, *who is repelled by an amulet bearing one of the mystical names of the archangel* Raphael."[19]

"Bring every thought to the obedience of Christ." Jonathan repeated the words over and over. "If anything stirs your spirit, you must test it against God's Word." He repeated the words again. What he could be sure of, so far, was this: the spirit known as "the Jezebel spirit" existed long before Ahab's wife and is still active; servants of Christ with the spirit of Elijah upon them must deal with the spirit to prepare the way for the Lord's coming; the end result of dealing with the spirit must be to restore the family unit, with godly men once again being godly husbands and fathers.

As he meditated, his knowing place was again illuminated. The worship of Baal included sacrificing children. Our children are being sacrificed still. **Children born out of wedlock, children born into families with absent fathers, are being sacrificed. Our society desperately needs to raise up godly husbands who understand the demands of a godly husband. Our children are not receiving the father's blessing and consequently they are seeking that blessing wherever they believe it can be found: sex, drugs, wealth, credit cards, new cars, bigger houses, bigger bank accounts, shinier jewelry, augmented breasts, tucked tummies.**

As Jonathan sat meditating on the message Raphael gave him that night while he slept, he remembered that Raphael said, "Learn the ways of the demon named Asmodeus and learn my purpose." Jonathan had already learned that Asmodeus was one of the fallen angels who sided with Lucifer, that Asmodeus was the demon of lechery, and that Asmodeus was associated with the female demon Lilith. Then he remembered that Lilith's offspring were called *Lilim* and he remembered *The Nephilim* of the flood in Genesis. He examined the passage in his Bible:

"Then the people began to multiply on the earth, and daughters were born to them. The <u>sons of God saw the daughters of men</u> and took any they wanted as their wives. Then the Lord said, 'My Spirit will not remain in humans for such a long time, for they are only mortal flesh. In the future, their normal lifespan will be no more than 120 years.'

<u>*In those days The Nephilim lived on the earth, for whenever the sons of God had intercourse with women, they gave birth to children who became the heroes and famous warriors of ancient times.*</u>

The Lord observed the extent of human wickedness on the earth, and he saw that everything they thought or imagined was consistently and totally evil" (Genesis 6: 1-5).

Jonathan knew that Hebrew legend claims the descendants of Cain coupled with fallen angels, and the result was giant monster-like creatures. The monster *Grendel* in the Old English epic *Beowulf* was supposed to be one of these offspring. One

thing is for certain: the *sons of God* who saw the "daughters of men" and married any of them they wanted, was the impetus that brought the flood. Jonathan also remembered that Raphael had said not to focus so much on the specific details of the legends, but on the truth behind the stories. When God says that "everything they thought or imagined was consistently and totally evil" one can conclude that at the very least, people were under the influence of evil forces. So Jonathan looked at *The Nephilim* a little closer.

One myth is variously developed in *The Apocrypha* and in *Midrashim* (a collection of early Jewish commentary on Biblical texts). In one story, two angels in confidence with God, *Semyaza* and *Azael*, were permitted by God to descend to earth to determine if man is worthy. When they arrived they were overcome with lust and begot monsters upon women. Semyaza repented; he was turned into the constellation called Orion by the Greeks. Azael (the demon in the Denzel Washington movie *Fallen*), far from repenting, still offers women ornaments, cosmetics and clothing so they can lead men astray. For this reason on the *Day of Atonement*, Israel's sins are heaped onto the annual scapegoat, which is thrown over the cliff to Azael.[20]

Genesis 6 does not present this episode as a myth, nor does it render judgment; it records the anecdote of a race of supermen simply to serve as an example of the increasing human malice that provoked God into sending the Deluge.[21]

The version told by the *Book of Jubilees* is that many of the sons of God were attracted to women. They decided to disobey God, descend to earth, and take women as wives. This act had many problematic consequences. It was a sin of hubris – a mixture of pride and lust. It also resulted in a mixture of the spiritual with the material, which was strictly forbidden by God. The sons of God imparted to their wives angelic knowledge not meant to be shared with humans, such as working enchantments and other magic.[22]

And once again, just as Jonathan was growing tired of examining myths, he noticed the name *Raphael* in the final paragraph of the page:

"The union between the angels and the daughters of Eve resulted in unnatural offspring. These Nephilim, or "fallen ones," were gigantic, destructive creatures. They required great amounts of food, and when food ran out they would eat humans and even each other. God sent the Great Flood to eliminate these abnormal beings and preserve the human race. However, there was a second occurrence of these creatures in Canaan, and Israel was charged with destroying them. The destruction was incomplete, and many got away, their fate unknown.

The fate of the rest of the Watchers *was to be held prisoner forever. Their leader, Azazel, was cast by the archangel* Raphael *into a dark pit (either in the earth or in the fifth heaven), where he will remain until Judgment Day, when he will be cast into the fire."*[23]

Once again, Jonathan became apprehensive. He believed himself following after stories that would have adverse effect on his walk with the Lord. And Raphael watched, and waited. As Jonathan sat in a haze, trying to makes heads or tails of what he was reading, and wondering if he was treading on dangerous ground where he did not have God's protection, Raphael was dispatched to earth and he whispered into Jonathan's ear: "Don't focus on the specifics of the story, but on the truth that lies behind the story." But I am supposed to bring every thought obedient to Christ, thought Jonathan. A demon being cast into a dark pit by an archangel? "Ephesians 6: 12," whispered the messenger:

"For we are not fighting against flesh-and-blood enemies, but against evil rulers and authorities of the unseen world, against mighty

powers in this dark world, and against evil spirits in the heavenly places."

Yes, thought Jonathan, but Azazel being cast in a dark pit, either in the earth or in the fifth heaven? "2 Corinthians 12: 2-4," the archangel responded:

"I was caught up to the third heaven fourteen years ago. Whether I was in my body or out of my body, I don't know – only God knows. Yes, only God knows whether I was in my body or outside my body. But I do know that I was caught up to paradise and heard things so astounding that they cannot be expressed in words, things no human is allowed to tell."

And Jonathan sat bewildered. What does it all mean and how does it relate to Solomon and Elijah and the rest of it? The drain in his skull was spinning again, sucking his brain down. And then he himself fell into some kind of vision. Where he was, he did not know. There was a light shining brightly, it was the color of sapphires and amethyst. Raphael's voice came through the light:

"The human language is not sufficient for expressing the deepest truths of the universe, the unseen realm of the universe. Just as Paul could not express in words what he saw, humans cannot express in words what their spirits know – in their knowing place – about the underlying truth of the human experience. That is why humans create myth and legend. Through symbolism and metaphor, humans come the closest they can to the unseen truth of the world. That is why Jesus, the Word made flesh, spoke in parables to his disciples, and why he said that "God is spirit, and his true worshipers must worship him in spirit and in truth." [24] That is also why Jesus said, "He who has ears, let him hear," [25] for it is only through your born again spiritual ears that you can understand the secret things of God. The Almighty's way of communicating to humans is in a way that will cause you to keep seeking him out. That is the only way he can get you humans to keep walking with him. Most of you, once you

think you know the truth, like children, think you can handle everything from there and you stray away from the Source of Wisdom.

Keep your eyes on the focal point. The Almighty has more messages to give you, but each of them will somehow bring you back to the first message. Solomon, son of David, was your first great king; Jesus, born from the lineage of David as far as his humanity is concerned, is the King of Kings and it is his kingdom that will last forever. Solomon's rule, like the Temple he built, came to ruin. And what was the purpose of the temple? To house the Holy Spirit of God. But Jesus, who came from God and who is God, is the true Temple of the Holy Spirit. What Solomon and his temple were unable to accomplish, Jesus accomplished in human form, though he is God. And you humans now are given the benefit of being the temple of God's Holy Spirit, and that is achieved merely by having faith in Jesus. How fortunate humans are, but still they treat lightly something so splendid.

Solomon failed because his heart was led astray and he bowed down in worship of foreign gods, which is idolatry. Human beings today are bowing down and worshiping false gods as well. Learn the truth behind the story! The abuse of credit cards is idolatry. The pursuit of money is idolatry. Pornography is idolatry. Abortion is no less bowing down to Molech than the Israelites sacrificing their children at the shrine of the detestable god. But all of these sins can be forgiven. Humans need only repent and put their faith in Jesus, and these sins are put away from you as far as the east is from the west; into the sea of forgetfulness.

The evil spirit that led Jezebel, and led Ahab, is the same spirit that led Solomon to his extravagance and the lust that turned his heart away from The Almighty. That same evil spirit is at work in the church today. God is calling servants to defeat Jezebel once again. Learn of her ways! Go back and learn of Asmodeus and learn my purpose! I am Raphael. I sit in the presence of The Almighty. Come. Elijah. All glory and honor to the Lord, Jesus Christ, forever and ever.

***

So back Jonathan went to his studies, with renewed zeal. First, he would finish the examination of Asmodeus. Then he would turn his attention to learning Raphael's purpose. As it seems always to go, the next piece of information which moved Jonathan's spirit he stumbled upon by chance. As he threw the last of the books he'd checked out of the library into the discard pile, he noticed a peculiar word: *Jinn*. He opened the book and read.

Islamic theology absorbed and modified the jinn; *some became beautiful and good-natured. According to lore they were created two thousand years before Adam and Eve, and are equal to angels in stature. Their ruler,* Iblis, *refused to worship Adam, and so was cast out of heaven along with his followers. Iblis became the equivalent of the Devil, and the followers became demons.*

As King Solomon fell deeper and deeper into his depravity, he came into contact with the evil spirits. Solomon, according to legend, used a magic ring to control jinn and to protect himself from them. With the ring, Solomon branded the necks of the jinn as his slaves.

One story tells that a jealous jinnee *(singular), sometimes identified as* Asmodeus, *stole Solomon's ring while he bathed in the river Jordan. The jinnee then seated himself on Solomon's throne at his palace and reigned over his kingdom, forcing Solomon to become a wanderer.*[26]

At this point Jonathan pondered. He believed he was beginning to understand what Raphael was trying to teach him. "Find the truth which lies behind the story." And it occurred to Jonathan that God was teaching him what had happened to Solomon - the same thing that happened to Ahab - and the same thing that is happening to potential men of God today. Asmodeus stole Solomon's ring while he bathed in the river Jordan, the very same river in which John the Baptist baptized Jesus. The ring represents the protection we have from Satan and his demons in Jesus. And Solomon, through lust, surrendered the protection he had from God when his heart was turned away from the Lord by worshipping foreign gods (idolatry). Consequently, Asmodeus represents the evil that sat on Solomon's throne while the man of God that Solomon once was had become a wanderer (like Cain when he was banished).

At this moment, the Holy Spirit reminded Jonathan of the passage in the first chapter of Romans:

"Yes, they knew God, but they wouldn't worship him as God or even give him thanks. And they began to think up foolish ideas of what God was like. As a result, their minds became dark and confused. Claiming to be wise, they instead became utter fools. And instead of worshiping the glorious, ever-living God, <u>they worshiped idols made to look like mere people and birds and animals and reptiles</u> **(and here the Holy Spirit illuminated Jonathan's knowing place: "This same thing is happening today, in your world.").**[27]

"So God abandoned them to do whatever shameful things their hearts desired. As a result, they did vile and degrading things with each other's bodies **("Your teens can watch these pornographic acts with ease on the internet.").** *They traded the truth about God for a lie. <u>So they worshiped and served the things God created instead of the Creator himself, who is worthy of eternal praise! Amen</u>* **("And you've already learned that this is idolatry, which runs rampant in the church today.").** *That is why God abandoned them to their shameful desires. <u>Even the women turned against the natural way to have sex and instead indulged in sex with each other. And the men, instead of having normal sexual relations with women, burned with lust for each other</u>* **("To tolerate this in the church is to tolerate Jezebel, which Jesus warns you about through his warning to the church in Thyatira.").** *Men did shameful things with other men, and as a result of this sin, they suffered within themselves the penalty they deserved.*[28]

"Since they thought it foolish to acknowledge God, he abandoned them to their foolish thinking and let them do things that should never be done. Their lives became full of every kind of wickedness, sin, greed, hate, envy, murder, quarreling, deception, malicious behavior, and gossip. They are backstabbers, haters of God, insolent, proud, and boastful. They invent new ways of sinning, and they disobey their parents. They refuse to understand, break their promises, are heartless, and have no mercy. They know God's justice requires that those who do these things deserve to die, yet they do them anyway" (Romans 1: 21-32).

Jonathan went back to the story about Solomon and Asmodeus, the evil spirit who sat on the throne while Solomon wandered in a state of depravity:

God compelled the jinnee to throw the ring into the sea, Solomon retrieved it, and punished the jinnee by imprisoning him in a bottle.

According to another story, Solomon brought jinn to his crystal-paved palace, where they sat at tables made of iron. The *Koran* tells how the king made them work at building palaces and making carpets, ponds, statues and gardens. Whenever he wanted to travel to faraway places, the jinn carried him on their backs.

Jinn appear in tales such as Aladdin's Lamp in Arabian Nights, in which they carry out the wishes of a master who learns magic that will command them. In Aladdin's Lamp, the genie imprisoned in the lamp is a derivative of the *jinnee* imprisoned in the bottle by Solomon.[29]

At this point, Jonathan came across a small passage that brought him a step closer to understanding what he was supposed to learn. The words elevated themselves:

In other lore, King Solomon, using his magic ring, forced Asmodeus and other demons to build his magnificent temple.[30]

And Jonathan immediately remembered Raphael's instruction: "Learn of Asmodeus and learn my purpose!" And his knowing place glowed. He understood that when Solomon allowed the worship of foreign idols he allowed evil spirits to inhabit the Temple. He also understood that it was sexual immorality which opened the door to Asmodeus (the demon of *lechery: unrestrained indulgence of sexual desire*). And Jonathan considered the consequences of a born-again Christian, who is the temple of the Holy Spirit, indulging in sexual immorality:

"*Run from sexual sin! No other sin so clearly affects the body as this one does. For sexual immorality is a sin against your own body. Don't you realize that your body is the temple of the Holy Spirit, who lives in you and was given to you by God? You do not belong to yourself, for God bought you with a high price. So you must honor God with your body*" (1 Corinthians 6: 18-20).

It was clear to Jonathan what must be done next. Raphael said, "Learn of Asmodeus and learn my purpose!" He rushed to the library to discover Raphael.

Raphael is one of the principal angels in Judeo-Christian angelology, accorded the rank of archangel. Raphael's name originates from the Hebrew *rapha*, which means healer or doctor, thus Raphael is "the shining one who heals"; also "the medicine of God." He is entrusted with the physical well-being of the earth and its human inhabitants, and is said to be the friendliest of the angels.

Raphael is counted among the seven angels who stand in the presence of God mentioned in *Revelation*. He is the guardian of the Tree of Life. In Kabbalistic lore, he is charged with healing the earth. He is believed to be one of the three angels who visit Abraham, though he is not named as such in Genesis. He is credited with healing Abraham of the pain of his circumcision, and Jacob of his wounded hip due to the fight with the dark adversary.

According to several rabbinic sources, a pearl hung on Noah's ark which indicated when day and night were at hand. Others say this light came from a sacred book Noah was given by the archangel Raphael, bound in sapphires and containing all the knowledge of the stars, the art of healing, and the mastery of demons. Noah bequeathed this to Shem, who passed it to Abraham. It went on through to Jacob, Levi, Moses, Joshua and Solomon.[31]

Then Jonathan dusted off a Bible that had set on his shelf for decades. It beckoned to him until he had no choice but to pick it up if he wanted the pull on his conscience to cease. He had known for some time that he would have to address this particular Bible. This Bible was distinct from the other seven Bibles contained in his personal library. He knew what this book held; a story about a man, a woman, a demon, and an angel who came to earth in the form of a man. The man: Tobias; the woman: Sara; the demon and angel: Asmodeus and Raphael. He was reluctant to investigate this story because it is contained in the Catholic Bible, in the section known as the Apocrypha. He was familiar with the Book of Tobit, which is considered canon by the Catholics, but not held in the same regard by Protestants, and not found in the Hebrew canon. Jonathan was in a quandary. Did he dare put faith in a book accepted as canon by Catholics, but not given the same weight by Jews and Protestants? He needed Divine counsel. He got down on his knees – a practice he'd learned while attending Catholic school for eight years – and beseeched the Lord for guidance.

And Raphael presented the prayer to The Almighty. And Raphael watched, and waited. And Raphael watched as Jonathan fell off to sleep. And the Healing Angel gazed into the brightness of one hundred million suns, and waited. Finally, he received his instructions and entered Jonathan's bedroom. The few demons that were lurking in the shadows, attempting to find whatever cracks in the armor that might show themselves, fled the moment Raphael's glory entered the room. They were all too familiar with the distinctive color of Raphael's armor...it shined with the brilliance of the spectrum of colors contained in a pearl, wrapped in the colors of sapphire and amethyst.

Raphael touched his charge on the forehead and Jonathan opened his eyes with a start. The light from Raphael's armor enveloped the room with a whiteness Jonathan had never seen. As Raphael touched his beautiful dreamer again, Jonathan bathed in a comfort inexpressible with human words. Raphael handed Jonathan his Catholic Bible and said, "Read. I will guide you to the truth." And Jonathan did as he was instructed.

Jonathan turned to the first page of the book. It read: *Presented to:* Deborah (**Jonathan's mother**). The next line read: *From: mother.* **And then in cursive:** *Esther Shaw, June 1961.* **Jonathan had never noticed this page before. "I was there when your grandmother gave this to your mother," said Raphael. "Your grandmother was visiting her oldest daughter, who was six months pregnant with you. And when your mother died ten years ago, I put it in your sister's heart to give this Bible to you, for that was God's will." Jonathan remembered what his sister said to him as she gave it to her older brother. "I don't know why," she said, "But I just feel like mom would want you to have this, Jonathan. Grandma gave it to mom the year you were born."**

Jonathan turned to the Book of Tobit and Raphael enlightened his seeker. The lesson lasted the entire night:

Remember, your task is to bring the ministry of Elijah back to the church in order to prepare the way for the Lord's coming. Luke, the beloved physician, has written that whoever has the spirit of Elijah upon him will "turn the hearts of the fathers to their children and the disobedient to the wisdom of the righteous." And this, dear pilgrim, is of utmost importance: it was not Elijah who killed Jezebel. Elijah's successor, Elisha, received a double portion of Elijah's spirit. Elisha then anointed Jehu King, and it was Jehu who killed the evil Jezebel. You, Jonathan, will not see the final coming of the Lord while you are alive on earth. It is your task to raise up godly husbands and fathers who will restore the wasteland that earth has become. And in the Book of Tobit, you can learn much about godliness. In the Book of Tobit, I will show you how the disobedient can return to the wisdom of the righteous, and you will also learn how to turn the hearts of the fathers to their children, which will raise up a generation of godly husbands.

You must understand the function of angels and you must know my purpose with you, so that none will be led astray by the evil one. In the 13th chapter of Hebrews, it is written, "Do not forget to show hospitality to strangers, for by so doing some people have shown hospitality to angels without knowing it."[32] And in the first chapter of the same book called Hebrews, it is also written, "Are not all angels ministering spirits sent to serve those who will inherit salvation?"[33] I am not to be worshiped or bowed down to, my purpose is to minister and serve those who will inherit salvation. Because of the sinful nature of flesh, which you have been consigned to on earth, you are unable to hear and follow the Holy Spirit continually and without fail, as the Lord Jesus was able to do during his sojourn on earth. Until the Lord comes again, to establish his kingdom forever, angels are assigned duties concerning God's elect. You are a dreamer and lover of heroic tales. Because of your nature, I have been assigned to you in order to help you understand the will and purpose of The Almighty. Whatever you hear from me, must be brought to the obedience of Jesus, who IS THE WORD OF GOD. It is imperative that you also understand I am not a hired hand to be ordered here and there by you, even though at the end of time, you will sit in judgment of even me. If humans understood the love God has for you and the place of honor reserved for you in all creation, there would not be need for angels such as myself descending to earth, either as celestial beings or in the disguise of human form until our mission is finished. You must never forget that my sole purpose is to bring God's healing to earth until Jesus returns. The wasteland in which humans live at present can only be healed through restoring the sacredness of marriage and the claiming of spiritual authority on earth by godly men.

I have been sent here that you may learn the truth within the Book of Tobit, which if applied to the situation in the church today, will bring healing to the body of Christ.

Tobit was born into the tribe of Naphtali, Israel's sixth son. Even though he was made captive by the Assyrian king, Tobit never failed to observe God's laws and he was faithful in giving alms to the poor always. When Jeroboam, ancestor of Ahab, made his detestable golden calves, Tobit fled the company of those evildoers and adored the Lord God of Israel in the temple at Jerusalem **(and you, man of God, must flee the idolatry which occurs even within the body of Christ today)**. *Tobit never failed to bring his tithes to the Lord and gave to the poor whenever he could. When it came time to take a wife, Tobit married Anna of his own tribe* **(men of God must be diligent in marrying believers in order to guard their hearts from turning away from the Lord, for this is the easiest and surest way for Jezebel to gain a foothold)**. *Anna bore Tobit a son and he named him Tobias, and Tobit took great care to teach Tobias to fear the Lord.*

Now it happened one day that as he was sleeping, hot dung fell out of a swallow's nest upon his eyes and made him blind. This trial the Lord permitted to happen to him, so he might serve as an example of patience, as also was holy Job. And as he had always feared God from his infancy, he uttered not a word against God for his blindness, but continued immovable in the fear of God, giving thanks to God all the days of his life.[34]

At this point Raphael stopped suddenly and looked toward heaven. "I am reminded of Gibran, the seeker from the hills of Lebanon, and his discourse on prayer," the angel said, but he wasn't speaking to Jonathan. "May I share his words here, my

Lord?" Raphael whispered. Jonathan shuddered as he realized the Healing Angel was speaking to God himself. Raphael bowed his head and continued his lesson to Jonathan.

*The poet from Lebanon once wrote, "**And if you cannot but weep when your soul summons you to prayer, she should spur you again and yet again, though weeping, until you shall come laughing. I cannot teach you how to pray in words. God listens not to your words save when he himself utters them through your lips.**"* [35]

Tobit never cursed or questioned God in his blindness, he only continued to praise God continually. At his moment of severest suffering, he began to weep and pray. This is his prayer that I presented to The Almighty on his behalf: "Thou art just, O Lord, and all thy judgments are just, and all thy ways mercy, and truth, and judgment. And now, O Lord, think of me, and take not revenge of my sins, neither remember my offenses, nor those of my parents. For we have not obeyed thy commandments, therefore are we delivered to spoil and to captivity and death, and are made a fable and a reproach to all nations, amongst which thou hast scattered us. And now, O Lord, great are thy judgments, because we have not done according to thy precepts, and have not walked sincerely before thee. And now, O Lord, do with me according to thy will, and command my spirit to be received in peace, for it is better for me to die than to live." [36] *You see, Jonathan, the same as Elijah and yourself, Tobit had come to the edge, he had come to the crags of despair. But the Lord is closest to his servants when they are weakest.*

Now it happened that on the same day, Sara, daughter of Raguel, in Rages a city of the Medes, was ridiculed by one of her father's servant maids. This woman Sara had been given to seven husbands, but Asmodeus, the demon of lechery, killed each of them before they entered her chamber to consummate the marriage. It is the goal of that wretched demon to sabotage new marriages. The servant maid said to Sara, "May we never see son or daughter of thee upon the earth, thou murderer of thy husbands." At these words, Sara went into the attic of her house; and for three days and nights she neither ate nor drank, but continued in prayer with tears, asking God to deliver her from this reproach.[37]

And now, Jonathan, I shall recite to you the prayer of Sara that I presented to The Almighty on the third day of her fasting. Listen and learn from the faithful servant: "Blessed is thy name, O God of our fathers: who when thou hast been angry, wilt show mercy, and in the time of tribulation forgives the sins of them that call upon thee. To thee, O Lord, I turn my face, to thee I direct my eyes. I beg, O Lord, thou loose me from the bond of this reproach, or else take me away from the earth."[38]

Now, Jonathan, pay close attention to the remainder of her prayer, for if applied to the church today, it could greatly advance the cause of the Lord: **"Thou knowest, O Lord, that I never coveted a husband, and have kept my soul clean from all lust. But a husband I consented to take, with thy fear, not with my lust. <u>And either I was unworthy of them, or they perhaps were not worthy of me, because perhaps thou hast kept me for another man</u>.** *For thy counsel is not in man's power. But this everyone is sure of that worship thee, that his life, if it be under trial, shall be crowned; and if it be under tribulation, it shall be delivered; and if it be under correction, it shall be allowed to come to thy mercy. For thou art not delighted in our being lost, because after a storm thou makest a calm, and after tears and weeping thou pourest in joyfulness. Be thy name, O God of Israel, blessed forever."*[39]

I can assure you, Jonathan, I have never presented a worthier supplication to The Almighty in the history of mankind. Both the prayer of Tobias and of Sara were heard in the sight of the glory of the Most High God, and I was sent to heal them both.

Meanwhile, Tobit believed his prayer was heard that he might die, so he called Tobias to his side. He instructed Tobias to go to Rages of the Medes in order to find a wife for himself. Tobit made his son swear that he would not marry a wife from the foreigners among whom they lived. So Tobias swore to his father that he would travel to Rages and find a woman from among their kinsmen to marry **(and you must do the same, Jonathan, although you are in the world, you are not of**

the world, and will suffer greatly should you marry a worldly woman who has not the Lord first in her heart).

But Tobias did not know the way to Rages, so his father bid him to find a trustworthy man for hire to take him there. Then Tobias went forth and found me, disguised as a beautiful young man, standing girded and ready to walk. And not knowing that I was an angel of God, he saluted me and said, "From whence art thou, good man?" I answered: "Of the children of Israel." And Tobias said to me, "Knowest thou the way that leadeth to the country of the Medes?" And I answered: "I know it, and I have often walked through all the ways thereof, and I have abode with Gabelus our brother (Sara's uncle), who dwelleth at Rages a city of the Medes." Then Tobias begged me to come with him to his father.

We entered Tobit's room and Tobias explained that I could take him to Rages. Tobias said to me, "Please, conduct my son to Gabelus at Rages and when thou shalt return, I will pay thee thy hire." I assured Tobit that I would take his son safely to Rages of the Medes. The next day, Tobias bid his mother and father farewell, and we set out together.

We lodged the first night by the river Tigris. As Tobias went to wash his feet, a large fish came up out of the water. Tobias was overcome with fear, but I took the fish by the gill and set it on the bank of the river. I instructed Tobias to take out the entrails of the fish, and lay up his heart, and his gall, and his liver, for these are necessary for useful medicines. I then explained if he put a little piece of its heart upon coals, the smoke thereof drives away all kind of devils, either from man or from woman, so that they come no more to them. And the gall is good for anointing the eyes, and they shall be cured.

I then explained to Tobias that we were looking for a man named Raguel, who had a daughter named Sara, and that he must ask Raguel for Sara's hand in marriage. Then Tobias answered, "I hear that she hath been given to seven husbands and they all died. Moreover I have heard that a devil killed them. Then I explained to him – **as I now explain to you** *– who they are that the devil can prevail over.* **_It is they who in such manner receive matrimony, as to shut out God_** *from themselves and from their mind, and give themselves to their* *lust, as the horse and mule which have not understanding, OVER* *THEM THE DEVIL HATH POWER..* [40]

Solomon gave himself over to lust, and eventually that caused him *to shut God out of his mind, which gave the devil power over him.* *Jonathan, remember Cain and the counsel God gave him. The Almighty* *said to Cain:* **"You will be accepted if you do what is right. But if** **you refuse to do what is right, then watch out!** Sin is crouching **at the door, eager to control you. But you must subdue it and be** **its master"** **(Genesis 4: 7).** *Listen to me, Jonathan, Abel pleased the* *Lord, but Cain did not learn how to master sin. Learn the difference* *between the two brothers, for they each represent a different covenant with* *God. Cain represents the Law; Abel represents the covenant sealed with* *the blood of the Lamb of God. It is by faith, not works, that Abel pleased* *God and overcame evil. But heed this warning: the Lord's brother himself* *wrote,* **"Faith by itself isn't enough. Unless it produces good** **deeds, it is dead and useless"** **(James 2: 17).** *You see, Jonathan,* *Abel was shown to be right with God by his actions when he offered the* *finest of his flock. It was his actions that made his faith complete.*

And remember Simon called Peter. Recall what the Lord said to *Peter as his sacrifice drew near:* **"Simon, Simon, Satan has asked** **to sift each of you like wheat. But I have pleaded in prayer for** **you, Simon, that your faith should not fail. So when you have** **repented and turned to me again, strengthen your brothers"** **(Luke 22: 31, 32).** *And what did Peter write about the devil? His* *words echo The Almighty's words to Cain:* **"Stay alert! Watch out for** **your great enemy, the devil. He prowls around like a roaring** **lion, looking for someone to devour. Stand firm against him,** **and be strong in your faith"** **(1 Peter 5: 8, 9).** And now back to the Lord's brother, who gives counsel on how to overcome: **"So** **humble yourselves before God. Resist the devil, and he will flee** **from you. Come close to God, and God will come close to you"** **(James 4: 7, 8).**

As I explained to Tobias who it is the devil has power over, he applied his heart to the lesson I taught him, for he was a righteous soul. Now I bid you to apply your heart to the same lesson that served Tobias so well. I instructed Tobias that before he and Sara married, he was to go with her into the chamber, and for three days keep himself continent from her, and give himself to nothing else but prayer with her. Learn the truth that lies behind the story, Jonathan. For three days he was instructed to give himself to nothing but prayer with Sara, and to keep from laying with her.[53] *Three is the number of spiritual perfection, and thus, the man and wife must be one in spirit, before their two bodies become one. As The Almighty ordained with the first husband and wife:* **"This explains why a man leaves his father and mother and is joined to his wife, and the two are united into one" (Genesis 2: 24).**

When we arrived at the house of Raguel, he welcomed us with joy. He quickly remarked that Tobias resembled his cousin, Tobit. I informed Raguel that Tobias was indeed his cousin's son. When Tobias made his wish to marry Sara known, Raguel became fearful because of what had happened to the seven husbands before. So I put him at ease, saying to him: "Be not afraid to give her to this man, for he is a man who feareth God, and God has set her apart to be the wife of this righteous man since before the world began, therefore no other man could have her."

Then Raguel said, "I doubt not but God hath regarded my prayers and tears in his sight. And I believe he hath therefore made you come to me, that this maid might be married to one of her own kindred, according to the Law of Moses." And taking the right hand of his daughter, he gave it into the right hand of Tobias, saying: "The God of Abraham, and the God of Isaac, and the God of Jacob be with you, **_and may he join you together_***, and fulfill his blessing in you."* **(You see, it was God who joined them together, not their own lust).** *And taking paper they made a writing of the marriage. And afterwards they made merry, blessing God.*

And then I explained to Tobias how to expel the demon Asmodeus. On the first night, he must lay the liver of the fish **(the fish representing**

61

Jesus) *on the fire, and the devil will be driven away. On the second night he and Sara would be admitted into the society of the holy patriarchs. And on the third night, Tobias must offer up prayers and supplications to the Lord, in order to cover his household with the blessing of Abraham.*

And after they had supped, they brought in the young man to her. And Tobias, as I had instructed him, took out of his bag part of the liver, and laid it upon the burning coals. Then Asmodeus fled and I pursued him to the desert of Upper Egypt where I bound him.

*Then Tobias exhorted the virgin, and said to her: "Sara, arise, and let us pray to God today, and tomorrow, and the next day, because **for these three nights we are joined to God, and when the third night is over, we will be in our own wedlock**. For we are children of saints, and **we must not be joined together like heathens that know not God**."*

And on the third night, Tobias offered up this prayer: "Lord God of our fathers, thou madest Adam of the dust of the earth, and gavest him Eve for a helper. And now, Lord, thou knowest that not for fleshly lust do I take Sara to be my wife, but rather for love that thy name be blessed forever and ever."

As we departed Rages and began our journey back to Tobias' home, I instructed Tobias to take with him the gall of the fish **(the fish representing Jesus)** *because it would be necessary in order to heal his father's blindness. I said to him: "As soon as thou shalt come into thy house, forthwith adore the Lord thy God; and giving thanks to him, go to thy father, and kiss him, And immediately anoint his eyes with this gall of the fish, which thou carriest with thee. For be assured that his eyes shall be presently opened, and thy father shall see the light of heaven, and shall rejoice in the sight of thee."*

Tobias did as I instructed upon our returning to the house of Tobit, his father. And after about half an hour, a white skin began to come out of his eyes, like the skin of an egg. And Tobit took hold of it, and drew it from his eyes, and immediately he recovered his sight. And they glorified God, both he and his wife and all that knew him. And Tobit said: "I bless thee, O Lord God of Israel, because thou hast chastised me, and thou hast saved me; and behold I see Tobias my son."

Then Tobit called Tobias and asked his son about me, "What can we give this holy man, who is come with thee?" Tobias answering, said to his father, "Father, what wages shall we give him? Or what can be worthy of his benefits? He conducted me and brought me safe again; he caused me to have my wife, and he chased from her the evil spirit. Thee also he hath made to see the light of heaven; and we are filled with all good things from him. What can we give him sufficient for these things?"

They had agreed to give me half of all their possessions, but when they called me aside, I said to them secretly, "Bless ye the God of heaven, give glory to him in the sight of all that live, because he hath shown his mercy to you. For it is good to hide the secrets of a king, but honorable to reveal and confess the works of God. I reveal then the truth unto you, and I will not hide the secret from you. When thou didst pray with tears, I offered the prayer to the Lord. And because thou was acceptable to God, it was necessary that temptation should prove thee. And now the Lord hath sent me to heal thee, and to deliver Sara thy son's wife from the devil. For I am the angel Raphael, one of the seven, who stand before the Lord."

When they heard my true identity they were both besieged with fear and fell face down on the ground. So I said to them, "Peace be to you, fear not. For when I was with you, I was there by the will of God. Bless ye him, and sing praises to him. It is time now that I return to him that sent me; but bless ye God, and publish all his wonderful works." And when I had said these things, I was taken from their sight, and they could see me no more.[41]

And Raphael departed from his dreamer's dwelling just as the orange glow of the sun crept over the eastern horizon. And Jonathan robotically performed the mundane tasks of the day that brought him the currency necessary to maintain his earthly existence. Jonathan was asleep fifteen minutes after entering his home that night. He didn't even bother with dinner. He now

had first-hand realization that, indeed, man does not live on bread alone, but on every word that comes from the Lord. And while he slept the Holy Spirit fanned the flame of the passion God had deposited in the dreamer upon his birth.

As soon as Jonathan mustered enough energy to roll out of bed, he set himself to discovering the requirements of a man with the spirit of Elijah upon him in the twenty-first century. This is what he discovered:

- **He must be willing to let God crucify his flesh:** *The flesh and its patterns must be subjected to the Holy Spirit daily in order for the person to be permanently set free.*
- **The Lord entrusted Elijah with the responsibility of raising up a generation that could stand and passing the baton to them to eliminate Jezebel:** *It was not Elijah who actually killed Jezebel. His disciple, Elisha, received a double portion of Elijah's spirit. Elisha then anointed Jehu king, and it was Jehu who actually killed Jezebel.*
- **Elijah was a vessel prepared in the wilderness of prayer and fasting:** *The wilderness of preparation cannot be bypassed or neglected.*
- **He must have no tolerance for Jezebel and her ways.**
- **He must stand in unwavering agreement with Jesus and His Word:** *We live in an hour that is pressuring the church to water down the message to be politically correct and inclusive to all. We accept all people, but not sin.*
- **He must embrace repentance and crucify the flesh:** *Galatians 5: 24 – "Those who belong to Christ Jesus have nailed the passions and desires of their sinful nature to his cross and crucified them there."* **The embracing of death will lead to life. Repentance solidifies his stance with Jesus in truth.**
- **Intimacy:** *The aim of the enemy is to allure us from pure devotion to Jesus as His bride. 2 Corinthians 11: 3 – "But I fear*

that somehow your pure and undivided devotion to Christ will be corrupted, just as Eve was deceived by the cunning ways of the serpent."

- **Consecration is a crucial dimension to overcoming:** *John the Baptist was a Nazarite who separated himself from the ordinary to be used by God for the extraordinary.*[42]

And as Jonathan finished the most recent entry in his notebook, the Healing Angel glanced into the brilliant rays of light cascading in never-ending and ever-increasing luster. Raphael knew what true consecration looks like, and he was acutely aware of how ignorant Jonathan was, at present, to the punishing hardship that awaited him. It was not Raphael's place to question the motives, or the methods, of The Almighty – he'd witnessed first-hand the consequences of an angel questioning God – and still could not comprehend the impetus that propelled the fallen ones who sided with Lucifer. So Raphael watched, and waited. He waited for the collapse which must inevitably come to the naïve knight whose consecration was imminent.

PARABLE II

Paul

"It is written," Jonathan's best friend and mentor said to him. **The friend, who was two years older than Jonathan, which also made him Jonathan's mentor, stood at the base of a cedar tree.** *The friend pointed to the top of the tree, which was barren.* "It is written. We must never touch the top branch of the tree."

As Jonathan stood looking at the top branch of the barren cedar tree, he suddenly found himself standing alone. He became frightened as an ominous storm began to approach from the horizon to the East (the Holy Land). The storm was furious and dark. Then he saw something coming toward him, an entity, bringing the storm with it. The fear grew within as the entity came into view. It was a black horse galloping toward him, and on the horse was a rider dressed in black, and the rider brought with him the storm.

Overcome with fear as the rider approached, Jonathan began to climb the tree in an attempt to escape the impending doom. The rider came to a halt at the base of the tree and pointed to Jonathan's feet. Without realizing it, Jonathan had climbed onto the top branch – the very branch his friend had warned him they must never touch. As Jonathan looked down at the branch, it broke and Jonathan fell to the ground. The branch remained attached to the tree by merely a sliver. Jonathan quickly attempted to repair the branch, and in doing so, *severed the branch from the tree completely. The fear within seemed uncontainable. Suddenly, the storm and the rider disappeared, and Jonathan found himself alone again.*

At that moment the apostle Paul appeared before the frightened young man. The apostle had with him a pack-horse, prepared for a long journey. "You must come with me now," Paul said. Jonathan was afraid. Somewhere – in his knowing place – Jonathan knew that if he went with Paul, he could not have a wife, which terrified him. **Jonathan was twenty-four years old at the time, and since he was fifteen had been praying for God to make him "the best husband and father in the world."**

"If you come with me," Paul said, "These three gifts will be yours." Paul held out three gold necklaces. "The first gift is Compassion. The second is Justice." Then Paul set those necklaces aside and held up the third. "This last gift, I have decided to give you. You can either use this gift or neglect it, the choice will be yours." Paul looked at the young man and a tenderness filled his countenance as he said, "This last gift is the ability to guide others."

Jonathan was afraid. And not knowing either why or how, he went with the apostle.

Jonathan thought about his best friend, who was also his mentor, but was only two years older than he. And therein lies a fundamental problem itself. His friend met no criteria of being a mentor; his qualifications rested merely in the fact that he was two years older and possessed two more years of life experiences. But the elder had taken an interest in the younger when Jonathan was fifteen years old because of talent he was gifted with in athletics. And so it came to pass that the elder stepped into the vacancy left by Jonathan's absent father.

Jonathan shot out of bed when the reality of the physical world crashed through the walls of his trance in the form of an

alarm clock. Lucky for him, though, he had a meeting scheduled with the priest later that day.

"This friend in your dream," the holy man said from across the desk, "He obviously has significant influence with you." Jonathan nodded in the affirmative. The rotund priest sat back in his chair and stroked his unkempt beard with his thumb and forefinger. "I want to address the tree first," said the priest.

"The tree in your dream is the Tree of Life. Or, more specifically, the tree of *your* life." Jonathan sat and listened. "The top branch represents what you want most in life." The priest leaned forward and asked, "What is it that you want most in your life, Jonathan?"

"A wife," the young man replied.

"I see," the priest said as he leaned back. "You'll need to figure out how this friend of yours has influenced you in the area of marriage." Then Jonathan noticed a hint of apprehension in the robed minister of God. After some silence, the priest added, "As far as the black horse and the rider dressed in black, you will find your answer to that in the Book of Revelation."

The church secretary knocked on the door and said from the other side, "Your six o'clock meeting is here, father." And with that Jonathan excused himself and made haste to his home in order to peruse that strange section at the end of his Bible that was treated like an attic to which someone had lost the key.

Revelation 6: 5, 6 – "When the Lamb opened the third seal, I heard the third living creature say, 'Come!' I looked, and there before me was a black horse! Its rider was holding a pair of scales in his hand. Then I heard what sounded like a voice among the four living creatures, saying, 'Two pounds of wheat for a day's wages, and six pounds of barley for a day's wages, and do not damage the oil and the wine!'"

Jonathan sat bewildered and unable to interpret the meaning at the moment. It would be many years - twenty-seven actually - before he would learn to accept the meaning through the crucible of experience. And Raphael gazed into the brightness again, himself perplexed. And just then the Healing Angel felt the warmth of love; not a warmth which collides into the nervous system from something external, but, rather, a serenity which overflows from within. And Raphael knew from whence came this feeling. The Lord Jesus had turned to look at the angel. "I have much to explain," the Lord said. "I will teach you what must take place in order for Jonathan to fulfill his role on earth. And when the time comes, you will help him as you have done several times already." And so Jesus enlightened the Healing Angel. The Lord and Raphael discussed the matter thoroughly:

"I remember the day you pulled young Jonathan from the irrigation ditch he'd fallen into on his grandfather's farm," the Lord said.

"Yes," said Raphael. "He was barely two-years-old at the time. His poor father thought the child had drowned."

"But you moved the father's arm, which hung paralyzed out of fear, to snatch the boy out from the rushing water and accompanied the father as he carried the boy into the farmhouse."

"Ay, and the father told grandmother that Jonathan was dead, but I whispered in her ear and guided her through the resuscitation."

"And since that day, Jonathan has had a susceptibility to pneumonia and an affinity for nurses."

"What you say is true, Lord."

"Jonathan has now received the second of four dreams he will be shown concerning his purpose on earth. In this latest vision, he has been given understanding of the consequences when a boy grows up in

a home with an absent father. And while he has not become an alcoholic like both of his parents were, he has inherited the addictive personality all the same."

"The Almighty spared him this burden, at least? Spared him the agony of being a prisoner of substance abuse?"

"He's not been spared anything. He has suffered ten times over the agony of being a child raised by alcoholics, with the added yoke of not having the luxury of medicating the pain himself. He's endured the emotional avalanche with nothing more than his own devices. His parents suffer the effects of the disease physically, he carries the scars of their disease in his memory. He's not able to live simply in the needs of today, he's not found the gift of forgetfulness."

"Does he remember still the night his mother came home at 2:00 in the morning, after she'd been unfaithful to his father?"

"Yes, he remembers it, while the episode has long since been wiped away from the consciousness of his older brother. His older brother's ability to erase the episode from his thoughts, while it didn't allow him to escape the event entirely unscathed, at least allowed him to move forward with his feet connected to the earth."

"His feet connected to the earth?"

"Yes. The older brother escaped some of what Jonathan could not, partly because he was sleeping in the top bunk. The violence occurred just two feet away from Jonathan because he was in the lower bunk. Ironically, older brother's viewpoint – which was from above – spared him the depravity in its entirety. And because older brother was a witness from above, he was able to remain grounded."

"And because Jonathan watched the sin take place from the floor, where it was perpetrated, his only coping mechanism was to rise above it all in his mind."

"Correct. Jonathan's viewpoint while it was taking place forced him to ascend above it all. He took flight that night, because he had no other means of coping with the fallout of the carnal explosion. Like Peter Pan, he flew to Neverland, where he could shape a reality of his own making. A reality where his father was justified in tearing mother's pants off; where father was exonerated for crashing through the boundaries that had long ago ceased to exist for mother; a reality where the void on his mother's face and the deadness of her eyes were transformed into guilt – her guilt – because the image he had created of father could not be tarnished, much less shattered by the vile and putrid act. It was all her fault because she had been with the railroad workers that night and she forced dad into his manic craze."

"And the result of his flight to Neverland was his being stuck emotionally. His feet were never grounded to the earth. He created a reality where he could survive, but that reality was false."

"That is correct. He is in need of much repair. The dreams will help him advance, in stages, back to earth and into society where he can become a vessel for the healing of others."

"And he will eventually have to deal with Abby, won't he?"

"Yes, but that won't come for years. There are other issues that need to be addressed before he can visit the years he spent inside the mist of despair. That relationship shaped more of his adult life than he can realize at present, but he will arrive at a place of rest from that pain in due time."

"Will he be punished for what happened when he is able to understand his sin in the matter?"

"No. But he will have to confess his part. He has blamed Abby and her parents all these years, but he will come to understand his own culpability."

"I remember watching him closely, as I was instructed, as he tried to medicate the pain with alcohol. And I remember his violent fits of vomiting. And I remember him being so hurt that he didn't even have the energy to cry out for God. His pain was so thick I could see it suffocating him as he tried to soothe himself through the caress of any female who would oblige him. And I remember him going to sleep at 7:00 in the evening, when the sun was still glowing with life, trying to shut his mind off so he wouldn't have to think about it."

"Remember how happy he was the day Abby told him she was pregnant?"

"Yes. He was so naïve then. He went to Lance's house and told him that he and Abby were getting married."

"Yes. It never even crossed Jonathan's mind to talk about it with his dad. He went straight to Lance, who was only two years his senior, but had filled the void left by Jonathan's absent father."

"And Lance gave him two hundred dollars to buy a wedding ring...so naïve."

"But so ready to believe in the impossible as well. He is a dreamer, yes, but when he has learned that with the dream comes the beginning of responsibility, he will move mountains."

"Will he meet his unborn son when the time comes for me to bring him home?"

"Christopher will be the first one to welcome him. But many things must take place before their first meeting. First, Jonathan must come to understand that, even though Abby's pregnancy was aborted, his son lives here with the Heavenly Father. Then, Jonathan must forgive Abby and her father for driving three hours east and keeping the procedure a secret from him. Then, he must find what has been the most difficult place in the universe for him to approach; he must find the mercy seat and realize that he has been forgiven. Before he can receive forgiveness for his sin of lust, he must come to understand that he is worthy of being forgiven. That's why the mercy seat remains hidden from him – he believes himself unworthy of being forgiven…unworthy of receiving mercy…unworthy of even being loved. It's never even occurred to him that Christopher, his unborn son, loves him. He has no idea that Christopher is proud of him."

"I remember how it crushed him every time his mother lashed out in anger at him. How she took out her anger on Jonathan because she found herself competing for her husband's affection with the child he favored. And I remember how Jonathan would fight to stay awake on summer nights so he could say goodnight to his father, who sometimes didn't come home until the early hours of the morning. And slowly he came to believe that he must win the favor of both his parents. He believed he must give them a reason to approve of him, a reason to love him."

"Yes, and he has carried that belief with him since. He believes it impossible for anyone to love him unless he gives them a reason, and his friend anchored that belief deep into his heart."

"But the fear of rejection was firmly rooted long before he met Lance, my Lord."

"That is correct. He felt rejected by his mother who resented him for being favored by his father. And even though his father treasured him

above everything else, because his father remained distant he believed he must still win his father's approval."

"What must he learn from the second dream, then?"

"In the dream, Lance, who had taken the place of Jonathan's father, said they were forbidden from touching the top branch of the tree. The tree represents his personal Tree of Life. Since Adam and Eve were banished from The Garden, and you were sent to keep them from returning to the Tree of Life, each person has their own tree. The top branch represents the one thing in life that person is willing to suffer for. The top branch is the desire which was placed in the person's heart while the Father knitted them together in the womb. The top branch is the area of life in which each person finds their highest capacity for compassion."

"Did you have a personal tree when you took on flesh and blood and descended to earth?"

"Of course."

"Of course, Lord. The one thing you were willing to suffer for. The salvation of mankind. Your passion."

"Correct. When Jonathan was fifteen years old, he began praying for God to make him the best husband and father in the world…"

"So naïve…oh, excuse me, Lord. Please continue."

"That is Jonathan's top branch. His greatest desire was to become a husband and father."

"But he is in his fifties now, and still has never been married. And the one child that carried his blood was never born."

"His request was no small thing to bring about. The father's curse has been passed through several generations, gaining power as it was transmitted from father to son in his family tree."

"And how does Lance fit in?"

"Lance came into Jonathan's life when he was fifteen. Jonathan has always put people on pedestals. He creates images of certain people in his mind and he gives those people far more power over him than they should have. It's also unfair to the person seated on the lofty perch, because they can't possibly live up to the image in Jonathan's mind. Eventually, when the person's humanity is revealed to Jonathan, he becomes disillusioned and desperately tries to place the person back atop the pedestal, which causes even more disappointment when he realizes this is an impossible expectation."

"So Lance replaced Jonathan's father on the pedestal."

"And Lance came from a broken home himself. Being two years older than Jonathan, and by nature more cynical and practical, Lance transmitted into his protégé's psyche the logic and rationale of the world. He passed on to Jonathan a belief system which adheres to the practical, measurable, and predictable nature of the world."

"But didn't Jonathan need to be grounded? Didn't he need someone to bring him down from the clouds and establish his roots to the earth?"

"Definitely. If Lance hadn't come into Jonathan's life, our beloved would have gone down a path of destruction where dire calamity awaited. Because of his environment, Jonathan became one of the 'flying boys' if you will. He became one of the millions of lads trapped in the 'Peter Pan Syndrome.' Boys who get stuck emotionally and can't grow up."

"But it wasn't Jonathan's fault, Lord. He could not have survived in that home without spiraling upward and ascending above it psychologically."

"Of course. And being one who escaped to Neverland, but then reentering the real world through his wound – that is where his genius lies. With the spirit of Elijah upon him, Jonathan will help males reconnect to the Heavenly Father's will in regard to being husbands and fathers."

"Of course. That's why he had to remain without a wife and without children so long. Just like Abraham's calling was to be the father of many, but was without a son, the one thing he desired most, for one hundred years."

"Yes. And just like Abraham tried to achieve the promise through his own power, which resulted in Ishmael, whose descendants have been a thorn in the side of Isaac's descendants throughout the ages, Jonathan tried to bring about God's promises by way of his own will, which has resulted in catastrophe for him."

"Ah...you speak now of his need for control."

"Yes. Because the home he grew up in was completely void of control, absent of any kind of consistency, emotional or otherwise, he feels the need to control everything...his environment and the people in it."

"So how did Lance affect his beliefs?"

"When Lance decided to take Jonathan under his wing, which was brought about because of Jonathan's athletic ability, which further embedded Jonathan's belief that he must win the affections of others, Lance appeared to have everything Jonathan wanted. He had a beautiful girlfriend, who remained faithful to Lance even though her faithfulness was not

reciprocated; he was the best athlete in the school, which brought popularity that every fifteen-year-old like Jonathan covets; but most of all, Lance was confident. Lance didn't need others to like him, and that is the personality trait Jonathan desired most."

"So Jonathan emulated Lance."

"Yes."

"Jonathan wanted to be just like Lance...and lost his own identity in the process."

"Yes. Jonathan came to believe that being himself was not good enough. No one would ever love him just for who he is. He believed he must change who he is in order to be loved."

"And it all began when he was a child."

"That's right. Jonathan, like so many others, did not experience the stages of maturity intended by Father, their creator."

"The first stage is bonding with the mother, which he never experienced."

"Correct. Samuel, Father's courageous prophet, is an example of this. The healthy process includes the child bonding with, and then separating from the mother. Hannah, Samuel's mother, had been unable to bear children. Each year, she and her husband, Elkanah, traveled to the temple to offer sacrifices." [1]

"Yes! And one year she wept mightily and uttered a heartfelt prayer. I presented that prayer to The Almighty. She made a vow, saying that if God would bless her with a child, she would give him back to the Lord. She said that her son would be God's for his entire lifetime, and as a sign that he had been dedicated to the Lord, his hair would never be cut."[2]

"And she kept Samuel until he was weaned, which is the age of three. When Samuel was three-years-old, Hannah gave him back to the Father. The first three years of a child's life is crucial. The child should bond with the mother during the weaning period, but then the child should separate from the mother in order to mature in a healthy way. Some children bond during the first three years, but no separation takes place. People on earth call them 'mama's boys.' But some children never bond with the mother, as in Jonathan's case, which causes the child to be insecure, like Jonathan is."

"The next stage, then, is bonding with the father?"

"That is correct. And this stage is crucial for girls as well as boys. The boys begin to imitate the father during this period. They hit their plastic nails with their plastic hammers, just like dad does with his real hammer. And ask any four-year-old girl who she is going to marry when she grows up. She is very likely to say that she's going to marry her daddy. The boys and girls alike are looking for their father's blessing between the ages of three and eight. They receive their sense of worth and their sense of purpose from the father's blessing. And this blessing doesn't necessarily need to be verbal. Children during this time period need to know they are being admired by their father. They need to feel like their father is proud of them. If the child does not receive proper reinforcement from the father during this stage, insecurity will rule in their lives."

"And there needs be a separation from the father as well?"

"Yes. Children seek autonomy at about eight years old. But this is a precarious period. Children come into the world with the notion they are royalty. The parents, in most cases, treat the child as though they are the center of the universe until about the age of eight. Suddenly, the child goes through a traumatic shift here. The child is abruptly informed that they

are not to think of themselves as special, and, as a matter of fact, they must quickly adapt to the truth that they are just one of many. Their parents, and the teachers at school, begin to point out the child's flaws. Other kids begin to tease them about their big teeth or their big ears; and the funny way they pronounce certain words, which used to be so cute, is now a source of embarrassment. They lose their sense of wholeness, and they spend the rest of their lives trying to recover that magical sense of being whole, that sense of being golden. It is a period of transition that must be navigated through by trial and error. The child must lose their sense of being the center of the universe, must experience the brutality of life so to speak, so they can be connected to their inner genius – the part of them that truly is unique and truly does set them apart from the rest. All children get wounded in some way during this time period, and it is through this wound they will find what is great in them."

"My Lord, I recall the day you stayed behind at the temple while your parents set off for home. You spent three days in the temple, immersed in dialogue with the teachers. When your parents returned and your mother admonished you for frightening them, you replied by asking her a question."[3]

"And what was the question?"

"You asked her why she didn't know that you must be about your father's business. Is that the next stage of development?"

"Verily, and this is the stage most neglected in the 21st century. This is the stage people like Jonathan must restore before I return. I was twelve years old when I stayed behind at the temple. And Samuel was twelve when the Father called him into service after he'd spent nine years with Eli in the temple. The boys experience Bar Mitzvah at the age of thirteen and the girls participate in Bat Mitzvah when they are twelve."

"They become accountable for their own actions and bear responsibility for obeying the Law of Moses."

"And the parents are no longer held responsible for the transgressions of the child. This concept has nearly disappeared in America today. When Joseph and Mary returned to the temple and found me participating in the business of the adult males, they came to realize I had assumed my responsibility as a member of the community. Remember when Abraham and Ishmael underwent circumcision?"

"I surely do, Lord. It was I who nursed Abraham's wound."

"And how old was Ishmael when he was circumcised?"

"He was thirteen."

"Yes. And he carried with him a physical reminder that he was expected to obey the Covenant with God and be held responsible for his own actions. The Native Americans understood the importance in this rite of passage. They understood that a boy does not become a man without the active intervention of the adult males in the community. The adult males took twelve and thirteen-year-old boys down into the Kiva. They entered into the womb of the earth. Upon entrance of the Kiva, each boy was given a physical wound; a wound that would leave some kind of scar. It was a physical reminder to the initiates that they were no longer boys. The initiates were aware, under no uncertain terms, the community expected them to behave differently from that moment forward. The young males entered the womb of the earth as boys, but they emerged from the womb as young men."

"So how were their lives different when they came out?"

"The young man was given to an adult male as an apprentice and he learned a trade. Sometimes, as in my case, the young man learned a trade from his father."

"And how long did this stage last?"

"Three or four years."

"And what happened after this period of transition?"

"Now that he is seventeen, the young man must enter The Garden. And here is the area in which the most damage is being done to the Father's Kingdom on earth. This is when the young man is intended to learn what it means to be a lover. At present, young men are not learning this; instead, they are exposed to pornography and a culture of casual sex without any intention of commitment."

"It grieves me to see your tears, Lord."

"And this is where the earth is in need of much healing, angel. Jonathan was seventeen when he fell prey to that demon of lust. He had no weapons with which to fend off the onslaught. Where our beloved was in need of mature guidance, Lance, a child himself, stepped in because there was no one else. Jonathan suffered much because of it. It nearly cost him his life."

"I remember it all too well. What should this stage of maturity look like when done correctly?"

"Therein lies the problem. This stage cannot be traversed correctly unless the young man has been brought successfully through the stages that preceded. If the proper foundation has not been firmly established, the young man will flounder through this period and make decisions that have long-lasting consequences.

Jonathan has experienced things children are not equipped to handle. But he is, sadly, one of many. He's barely survived, but soon he will be ready to become a vessel through which healing can flow. He never bonded with his mother, which is not her fault any more than it is his. She suffered unspeakable tragedy when she was young as well. He will have to forgive her someday, if he wants to proceed. Then, between the ages of three and eight, when he needed to bond with his father, there was only the faint shadow of a man that passed through intermittently."

"He was six when his father raped his mom in front of him. As his father screamed about her sleeping with the railroad boys, Jonathan shifted the blame onto his mother in order to maintain the heroic image he'd created of his absent father. He was eight when he and his brother were wakened in the middle of the night to the sound of the furious storm that ended with his father in the hospital. Jonathan can still hear the sound of the kitchen knife entering and exiting the palms of his father's hands, as he raised them to protect himself over and over and over again. When his dad finally passed out in a pool of blood, Jonathan and his brother thought she'd killed him.

And when his mother and father returned from the hospital, dad's hands bandaged, along with the social worker, Jonathan began to hate his mother because his parents lied to him, his brother, and the social worker, saying this kind of thing would never happen again, as they stood there with their arms around each other as though they were in love."

"And Jonathan became a very sad boy. He was disappointed with his older brother for believing their parents' lies. But that could have been dealt with easy enough. Perhaps the saddest people in the world, though, are boys who hate their mothers."

"So Jonathan never bonded with his mother, never bonded with his absent father, never experienced initiation into adulthood accompanied by the active intervention of the adult males of the community, and never learned a trade. Then, when he was seventeen and should have been ready to learn how to cultivate Godly love for a woman, he became a victim of the world and got lost in the enchanted mist, where his girlfriend became pregnant and then snuck away to have an abortion. And his fear of rejection became so deeply seated in his psyche, there was no room for receiving genuine affection from any member of the opposite sex."

"And we still haven't even touched upon the incident that even you, dear healer, can bear to discuss."

"It grieves me so, dear Lord."

"Raise your head, messenger. Remember that Father works everything – even the heinous acts – out for the good of those who love him. And you know that Jonathan loves him."

"To watch it happen, without being given permission to stop it, Lord. It grieves me."

"But Jonathan had to experience it in order to understand how to help others. He will help others learn to restore boundaries one day. You saw my tears as our beloved boy, only twelve-years-old, lay beside his brother and their cousin, who were both two years older than our prophet. You witnessed as I uttered groans incomprehensible to human ears as the cousin, much bigger and much stronger, crashed through any boundaries that may have existed for Jonathan."

"I'm thankful that Almighty allowed me to wake Jonathan's brother, so he could stop the cousin...Please, Lord...Let us return to that incident, if it is imperative that we do so, after we've discussed the remaining stages of development for a male.

After the young man learns to become a holy lover, what is the next progression?"

"The young man, now about twenty-years-old, should learn what it means to be a warrior."

"But you were a man of peace, my Lord."

"That does not mean I wasn't a warrior. I had to be fierce in the arena of spiritual warfare. You know that, angel. You were one of those who came to my aid in the desert, after I'd waged war with The Tempter. Remember when Joshua led the Israelites into the Promised Land?"

"Certainly."

"None over the age of twenty were allowed to enter except Joshua and Caleb, after the twelve scouts returned from surveying the land, because the people did not trust the Lord to keep the promise he had sworn to Abraham; the promise to give his descendants the land inhabited by the Canaanites. And when it came time for Joshua to lead the people into the Promised Land, the Lord left behind the five rulers of the Philistines, the Canaanites, the Sidonians, and the Hivites who lived on Mount Lebanon from Mount Baal Hermon to the border of Hamath. The Father did this because the Israelites entering the land had never experienced war. The men entering to possess the land promised by Father had to be trained and skilled in war before they could settle in the land.

Any male who wishes to be a man and hopes to be worthy of being a husband, must learn the art of warfare. He must learn what it means to be a warrior. And a warrior is different from a soldier. The soldier ventures off to foreign lands and fights for his country. He then takes the spoils of war back to his community to share with his people. A warrior, however, draws a circle around whatever is his – including people – he then remains inside the circle and fights to the death to protect whatever is in the circle."

"I see, Lord. David, your human ancestor, was a mere lad of sixteen when Samuel first anointed him as future king of Israel. But it was not until he was thirty that he actually assumed the throne. At sixteen, he was a shepherd; he had not yet learned to be a warrior."

"Indeed. But learning to be a warrior is something much different today than it was then. Young men today are not called upon to defeat armies

of men; they must be equipped to defeat foes in the spiritual realm. It is not against flesh and blood they must wage war, but against the powers of darkness at work in the world."

"And I suspect the time period spent learning to be a warrior takes about three years as well?"

"When it is done correctly."

"So now – in the ideal situation – the young man is about twenty-two-years-old. What now?"

"Now the young man is ready to learn kingship. And he is ready now also to win the princess. After proving himself worthy of the love of the princess, the two shall be united and she will be his queen."

"So in the case of Jonathan, he's representative of how far the world has been led astray by The Evil One?"

"In many ways, yes. He's suffered things that many don't survive, because only by experience can humans learn certain kinds of pain. The same way I had to experience every temptation, and suffer mightily, and learn obedience through what I suffered, Jonathan will become a vessel of healing because of the pain he's had to endure."

"Back to the dream he received, Lord. He and Lance were at the base of his personal tree of life. And Lance said that it was written they could not climb on the top branch."

"Lance came from a broken home as well. His father was unfaithful to his mother, and Lance believed it was foreordained that he would become just like his father. And his belief did become a self-fulfilling prophecy. Lance was unfaithful as well."

"But Jonathan has never been unfaithful, Lord. Instead, he has become loyal to a fault."

"That is true. But Jonathan's hyper-loyalty is the result of his insecurity – an insecurity Lance never had. Lance repeatedly told Jonathan that a good marriage was beyond their grasp because they had such poor role models. Lance was Jonathan's idol. Whatever Lance told the impressionable teen, he believed without question."

"I see...and when Jonathan had finally recovered from the rejection by Abby, which took four years, he fell in love with the princess...the woman so perfect in his eyes that she became the one by which all others would be compared – and be found wanting."

"Elizabeth."

"And Elizabeth was from one of the wealthiest families in the county."

"And Jonathan's family was dirt poor."

"And Lance repeatedly told Jonathan that Elizabeth would never marry him because he came from a poor family. 'Elizabeth's family does not marry down,' and, 'The more money you have, the more attractive you will be to women,' and, 'It doesn't matter how nice you are. Women like Elizabeth only marry men in a certain tax bracket.'"

"And even though Elizabeth dated Jonathan for three years, she made it clear from the beginning she would never marry him."

"But he was lost in quicksand. He was, and still is all these years later, the best friend she ever had. Her husband, who comes from a family even wealthier than hers, will never know her as well as Jonathan did."

"Jonathan's relationship with Abby, and the way it ended, scarred him deeply. But the three years he spent with Elizabeth hurt him severely as well."

"He didn't have the ability to move on from Elizabeth, any more than he could let go of Abby. And we haven't even gotten to Katherine yet. But still, Elizabeth has remained, for thirty years, the one he refuses to relinquish...the one he will not allow to step down from the throne on which he has placed her."

"And you know why."

"Because she was a virgin."

"And she remains undefiled in his memory. You saw the way he slipped further and further into the downward spiral after Abby. He desperately sought love and approval, and he believed the lies of the world. He became convinced that being skilled in sexual intercourse could win him the worship of the female, which in turn would fill the emptiness in his soul; an emptiness that began when he was a small child and grew wider and deeper with each passing year and each young lady who was drawn to his spirit, but eventually broke his heart when they sensed his brokenness – a brokenness they could not define but also knew they couldn't fix."

"It was as though he fell into a whirlwind, and once inside, could not gain enough footing to escape."

"He went from damsel to damsel, and while he could win their worship through sexual means, he could not cure their distress. And the more sex they had, the tighter the damsel would cling, until completely unable to engage in true intimacy, he would tear away abruptly, lick the wounds caused by the separation, and pursue the next band aid to patch the ever-increasing wound."

"Until he found Elizabeth."

"He latched on to her ray of light and pulled himself out of the pit. They were both twenty-one, and she was a virgin. He had finally found a real-life princess. And she loved him, even though he was a mere commoner. But she saw in him the potential of royalty, however buried and dormant that potential was. She sensed his kingly quality in her spirit."

"All the boys she had dated, until Jonathan, eventually left her because she would not forfeit her purity until marriage."

"Yes. The others left her because she refused to surrender her chastity; and Jonathan loved her for it. She was the one pure, unsullied treasure in the mud-stained, cesspool his life had become."

"But, Lord. Didn't he end up worse for the experience? Didn't it send him, in the end, further into the dark forest?"

"It did. But it also brought him closer to his destiny. As much pain as it caused him, it was a necessary stage in his preparation for ministry."

"I remember the day Elizabeth made her final break, my Lord. The relationship had been such a rollercoaster. She loved him; that she knew. But she also knew she would never marry him. He simply wasn't stable enough; he wasn't even close to being a provider. Her parents liked Jonathan, but they never would have given their blessing to a marriage with him. So Elizabeth would break up with Jonathan, then about two months later, missing him desperately, she would ask him back. And poor Jonathan. He was so madly and hopelessly in love with her, that he had no choice but to drink in every moment with her the way the sun-parched dessert drinks in every drop of rain and holds on for dear life."

"And after three years, when the relationship had gotten to the point where they either needed to get married or move on, knowing that she couldn't marry him she took the one course of action she knew would make

the break complete. She dove into a relationship with a young man from a family of the same social status as her own. She did it because she knew that was the only way for her to sever the ties with definitive force."

"And that's when Jonathan first knocked on the door of Father Thomas. He'd come to the end of his rope. If he didn't find hope from somewhere, he couldn't go on. It was the first turning point in his life."

"So it was. That knock on Thomas's door began the process of Jonathan finding his way to the life the Heavenly Father intended for him."

"And now he had an influence in his life to counteract the influence of Lance and the world."

"Correct. Now I will inform you of what must take place for Jonathan to understand his purpose on earth. He will be led at times to the revelation by the Holy Spirit. But he will also close his ears to the Spirit at times which will cause him to flounder and flail. You, angel, will be called on to lead him through perils. You will even save him from death in an automobile twice. With the intervention you performed when he was drowning, and the two accidents that come later, you will save his life three different times. And he will be brought to the edge of suicide on two different occasions before he finally surrenders his life to me completely.

***

"The tree of Jonathan's life is barren. At present, when he draws near to the Heavenly Father, the motive in his heart is to curry favor with God, hoping the Heavenly Father will make his life better as a result of his good behavior. He is so steeped in the belief that love must be earned he is unable, at this time, to even comprehend the concept of grace, let alone the truth of the freedom available to him through the free gift of God. He believes, in his heart, that he must provide God a reason to love him; a reason to act on his behalf."

"And this belief comes from the manner in which he received love from his parents?"

"Yes. And many will attempt to convince him that his desire to earn grace through works is the result of being raised in the Catholic Church. Many discuss – and argue – at length the differences between Grace-based churches and Works-based churches. The truth is, a person's propensity to believe they must earn grace comes primarily from the manner in which that person's parents show approval and dole out love. If an earthly father loves unconditionally and disciplines in a way that reassures the child he still loves them, that nothing can separate the child from the love of their father, even though some actions require loving discipline, then the child, regardless of denomination, will be receptive to the truth of grace and God's gift."

"Please, Lord. Explain the dream to me in its entirety, and illuminate me in regard to my function in The Almighty's plan. I shall hold my tongue until you have revealed all in this matter."

"The tree of his life is barren because he has not learned to remain in me. It will take many years and he will suffer catastrophic setbacks before he finally learns that his works, attempted to win God's favor, are filthy rags in the Father's sight as long as they lack faith and dependence on me.

His need of approval and the pain he's suffered from his relationships with Abby and Elizabeth have caused him to believe the lies of the world. He has come to believe that his worth – and his attractiveness to any potential bride – rests entirely in his financial portfolio and the prestige he attains in his profession. The events in his life have convinced him that no one would – or could - love him simply for who he is. He will attempt, for twenty-seven years, to win the approval of his earthly father and the princess on the hill through becoming larger in the world's eyes and estimation. Elizabeth loved him mightily, and she could not conceal that love from his spirit. But the way in which she ended their relationship - according to that which was preordained doctrine in her family - and clung to the practical choice of men from her family's social status, has served to enshrine her as a real-life Daisy Buchanon in Jonathan's heart. And, much like the fictional Jay Gatsby, he clings to a false hope; a hope that somehow he can earn enough money and status to win the heart of the princess on the hill. And in his attempt to become the man Elizabeth would marry, like Gatsby, he has forfeited his own identity and come to despise the man God intended him to be. So he will create a façade. But his Heavenly Father will not allow him to live a false life, which will necessitate a complete tearing down of the image he works so hard to maintain and project to the outside world.

He will actually achieve a certain amount of success and win prestige in the eyes of the world, and he will be proud of himself. But he will never find the love of the princess, and his pride will indeed precede a devastating fall. He will attempt with all his strength and might to elude the financial destruction Father will bring upon him, to no avail. After he has fallen, and everything he has of worldly value – including the false status he believes he has achieved – has been taken from him, he will come to a place where he can finally understand the truth of his life.

In his dream, he finds himself on the top branch, but the branch becomes severed from the tree. And the branch is barren. Jonathan's greatest desire is to be a husband and father. That desire was put in his heart by The Creator. Indeed, only when a man and his wife are joined together do they reflect the full image of God. And because being a godly husband and father was placed in his heart, this is also the area of his life in which the Father will require him to be holy and honorable. But he will never be holy and honorable in Father's eyes until he has been shaped, through the fire of discipline and hardship, into my image.

Only when he has exhausted all of his own strength and wherewithal, and then been brought to a despair nearly unbearable – a despair which brings him to the very precipice of suicide at the edge of a razor blade – and after he has been stripped of every worldly possession (and, in truth, every distraction), will he be able to understand the truth about his life - his personal tree of life.

When he has been emptied of the contamination of the world, he will come to understand that I am the true vine and the Father is the gardener. He will learn through the pain of experience that Father cuts off every branch of mine that doesn't produce fruit, and he prunes the branches that do bear fruit so they will produce even more. The top branch in his dream represents his calling, which is turning the hearts of the fathers to their children. He comes from parents who were broken, which caused him to be broken as well. He tried to win the love of the princess through worldly means. His need for affection, and need for control, will be used by Satan and Jonathan will believe it is through sexual intercourse the love of the princess is won. He will be led by the deceit of Satan, like so many others, and will move to possess that which he loves. He will need to learn the ways of holy love.

In his dream, the top branch is severed from the tree. And that is because the Father is the gardener. Jonathan will come to a point where his desire to do the Father's will shall grow so strong, he will relinquish even the greatest desire of his own heart. His need to stay in the Father's will shall become stronger than his desire to be married and he will actually relinquish his desire to be married in favor of furthering the kingdom of God. When he comes to this point, he will be a tool worthy of honorable use and will become someone his Master can use for every good work. He will learn that a branch cannot produce fruit if it is severed from the vine, and that vine is me. And he will learn that he cannot be fruitful unless he remains in me.

The top branch in his dream was severed because he must come to understand that apart from me he can do nothing. His marriage can never receive the Father's blessing unless it is done according to Father's will. Jonathan has been chosen to help restore the sanctity of marriage. Our beloved had no idea what he was asking when he uttered the prayer that God make him the best husband and father in the world. The institution of marriage – the institution established by The Creator in The Garden – has nearly vanished on earth. And all creation eagerly awaits the day for God to reveal who his children are, because against its will, all of creation was subjected to God's curse. And the creation has been groaning as it looks forward to the day when it will join God's children in glorious freedom from death and decay.[4]

A world with absent fathers has produced many immature men like Jonathan. They have grown wings in an attempt to escape the profane characteristics of the world. Society without the father is producing these ungrounded men who become very intense and very charming; they become so sincere and so open to addiction. These men, when they are between the ages of seventeen and twenty-two, when their spirits yearn to enter the heavenly chamber in the King's castle, young men who should be learning what it means to be a holy lover and a holy warrior, are instead migrating to the singles' bar, which the world has fashioned to resemble the King's room. In these bars, the holy lover within these men becomes mingled with the sexual hunter inside. The hunter gains power as he makes extravagant promises of ecstatic visits and long stays in the heavenly chamber. The man's spirit endures losses during these needy unions.[5] And this still does not take into account the damage done to the female; the woman God has created specifically for a holy union with her husband.

Jonathan's initial dream gave him the revelation that Solomon was the first King to build God's temple. And he will learn that sexual immorality opened the door to the defilement of God's temple. In his second dream, after the top branch is severed, Paul arrives and invites him to come on a long journey. Paul has three GOLD necklaces to give Jonathan while he travels and learns from the apostle to the Gentiles. At present, Jonathan is still made of base metal. And these needy unions with women in the singles' bars is representative of the lesser wedding, which is the wedding Solomon presides over. The lesser wedding is a union, or fusion, of substances that are not yet thoroughly separated or discriminated. The lesser wedding is always followed by a death. The Great Wedding happens later.[6]

Jonathan will eventually succeed in finding the second King. The King who accomplished with God's temple what Solomon could not. The

King who established the everlasting temple. Jonathan will find his way to me, The King of Kings; the Alpha and the Omega. He will learn that even though he once thought he was rich - because he evaluated wealth according to the world's view - that he is, in fact, wretched and miserable and poor and blind. He will find that just like Adam in The Garden, he is naked. As he travels with Paul as his mentor, Jonathan will heed my advice and buy GOLD from me – GOLD that has been purified by fire. Then, when he has been stripped completely of worldly gain, he will be rich. And he will receive white garments from me so he will not be shamed by his nakedness. He will learn, painfully, that I correct and discipline everyone I love. And finally he will join me at my banquet table, he and his wife, and the two of them will become participants in The Great Wedding.

Jonathan must learn that anyone who does not remain in me is thrown away like a useless branch and withers. And that such branches are gathered into a pile and burned. But anyone who remains in me and my words in them, may ask the Father anything they want, and it will be granted. Just as Elijah called down rain on the earth, because he was in the Father's will, those who remain in me and follow my words will perform mighty deeds on the Father's behalf for the benefit of mankind. Anyone who produces much fruit is my true disciple. This brings great glory to the Father.[7]

And, through Paul's guidance, Jonathan will learn that I love him as the Father has loved me. He will learn that to remain in my love, he must obey my commandments; just as I obey the Father's commandments and remain in his love. He will learn that it was not he who chose me, but it was I who chose him. And he will understand that a man does not choose his calling; rather, it is his calling that chooses him. After all, what choice did Paul really have, lying blind on the road to Damascus? I have chosen him to go and produce lasting fruit, so the Father will give him whatever he asks in my name. Jonathan will learn from me, through Paul's writings, and he will put on the GOLD necklaces of Compassion and Justice. As his fruit increases, he will put on the GOLD necklace which gives him the ability to guide others. And this third necklace will be given him by the Holy Spirit, as the Spirit chooses, to build up and edify the church.

Jonathan is twenty-five years old at the moment. He has been wounded in the area of love and acceptance several times. His relationship with his mother has left him with a deep-seeded fear of rejection. His relationships with Abby and Elizabeth have scarred him deeply. Six months from now, he will enter into a relationship with Katherine. She is two years older than Jonathan and is the same age as Lance. Katherine is married and has a three-year-old daughter. When Jonathan meets Katherine, she and her husband will have been separated for several months, but their divorce will not yet be final. Katherine was the Winter Homecoming Queen at Jonathan's high school his sophomore year. And this is how he sees her still, ten years later. She will smile at Jonathan six months from now; he will be standing behind her about ten paces to the right. She will turn and they will make eye contact. She will smile with an inviting coyness that entraps the poor boy and he will be lost in the enchanted mist, again.

He will wait for her, as she knew he would, and the two will engage in a very superficial conversation. The next day, Jonathan will ask Lance about her, and Lance will tell him that she is separated from her husband. Lance will tell him that her husband has moved three hundred miles east, and that she has no intention of reconciling with him. One month after their initial conversation, Jonathan and Katherine will have sex on her living room carpet while her three-year-old daughter is visiting the father all those miles away. And Jonathan will sink deep into the mist. He will continue to sink until the voice of the Spirit is drowned out by the growl of lust. And this growl, born in the depths of his unregenerate loins, will come to sound like a symphony as Satan perverts reality.

And the boy, old enough to be a man – but isn't - will become lost in the mist, unable to even respond to the invitations of the Spirit.

And the boy, old enough to be a man – but isn't – will achieve status in the world's eyes. And the Evil One will fill the boy's mind with lies that puff up his opinion of himself. And the boy will become, at the age of twenty-five, the supervisor of men twice his age. And the Evil One will entice these older men of the world to flatter the boy. And the men will applaud Jonathan and tell him how they wish they'd been as gifted as he is when they were his age. And his business will take Jonathan to exciting places, where he meets exciting people. He will become so enamored with the pursuit of wealth and prestige, that he will spend more time traveling than he spends with Katherine. And he will come to despise the time he does spend at home. And he will dive further and further into the whirlwind. And eventually, he will become so depraved that he will find himself in a hot tub at the most expensive hotel in Jupiter, Florida, and as he sits in the hot tub, looking out on the beach, he will utter aloud the words, 'I don't need anyone else in the world.'

And these words will set in motion the rider dressed in black, riding the black horse. And the rider will bring with him the storm. And four months before his twenty-seventh birthday, he will fall from the false heights he has achieved. Within forty days of uttering his false prophecy about not needing anyone else in the world, he will have lost Katherine, his lofty position in the business world, and all of his money. He will go from being financially independent to being in debt, with no real prospects. And he will find himself in the office he can no longer afford in such a state emotionally, that he will caress the cold steel of a gun and welcome the nothingness it promises. He will then utter the plea, 'God, I know my church teaches that I will go to hell if I pull this trigger. But hell can't be this bad.' And then you, healing angel, will be sent to bring him the gift of sleep."

***

"Excuse me for interrupting, Lord. But you just said he will contemplate suicide with a gun."

"*Yes.*"

"But earlier, Lord, You said that he would seek relief at the edge of a razor blade."

"*Correct. The razor blade will be the second time he contemplates suicide.*"
"Of course, Lord. Please, continue."

"*Jonathan never received proper mentoring in his life. Paul, through his writings, will become that mentor. Jonathan will be twenty-seven years old when he begins his journey with Paul. Jonathan's mentor will tell him what to do with his wounds, and Jonathan will become what earth knows as 'The Wounded Healer.' With Paul as his guide, he will come to the Holy Water. He will learn to bow his head and live a secret life, praying in a closet. He will learn to be lowly, to eat grief as the fish gulps water and lives. He will learn to be active with his soul. As Paul brings him to the water, Jonathan will begin his descent from enchantment; he will begin the process of becoming grounded. In the presence of his mentor, Jonathan will learn where his genius lies. Eventually, the wounds that have nearly caused Jonathan to take his own life, he will regard as a gift. For the truth shall forever remain: Where a man's wound is, that is where his genius will be.*

One day, years from now, Jonathan will understand that he is the Father's son. He will come to understand that God the Father is the King he has been searching for his entire life. In order for this to happen, Jonathan must experience the road of ashes, descent, and grief. [8] *One day, Jonathan will realize that in following Paul, he was able to avoid the way of drug addiction and self-shaming. Instead of going the way of delinquency, Jonathan will be lifted up to what is great in him. The sad truth, though, is that in order for Jonathan to learn what he must, he will fall and experience humiliation. He will descend and make an exit from ordinary and respectable life through his wound – which will, in the end, heal him of his fear of rejection.* [9]

As I said earlier, the Father is the gardener, and this has been so since The Garden of Eden. Before Jonathan's helpmate can be presented to him, he must learn how to tend a garden as well. This shall be done in the spiritual realm, for it is Jonathan's spirit which must be healed. Jonathan will learn to love cultivation more than he loves excitement. This is the garden way. In the garden, he will cultivate yearning and longing, and he will begin to notice the tiny desires. Paying attention to small, hardly noticeable feelings is the garden way, and that's the way holy a lover behaves.[10]

Jonathan must advance to the place where love for God and the love of God floods through the self, out to God, and out to others. Then he will be able to love out of fullness, not out of need. He must advance to a place where he needs others to love in order to release the love of God that is in his heart, not to obtain the love he needs. At present, his love relationships become the expression of his immature desires: 'Let me do what I like. Give me what I want. Prove to me that I am somebody!' At present, when he says, 'I love you,' what he's really saying is, 'I want you; love me!' Then, because he has not matured emotionally, when the needy union crashes and burns, he says, 'I hate you for not loving me.'

Jonathan will learn - slowly, for his need to control whatever he loves is so great - not to awaken love prematurely, for love is very tender and easily harmed. At its own proper time it will awaken of itself. Love should not be stirred up before its proper time, because the love relationship, unless carefully guarded, may cause grief instead of great joy. Worthy love will awaken of itself in its own time.

One day, Jonathan will understand the desire of one who truly loves is so strong that he gives himself completely to the other and desires the same strong, exclusive affection in return. Such a love for another is from God the Father, who put it into man's heart, and it cannot be extinguished. Neither can it be bought. Not even Solomon, with all his wealth, could buy the love of the girl.

His journey will be long and arduous. He will learn much, and make great strides for about five years. But his wounds are many. He has the spirit of Elijah upon him, which means he also has adversaries in the spirit realm. As he comes nearer to his calling, he will attract demons, dormant complexes, and bitter enemies of the spirit.

Jonathan will receive words of knowledge from the Holy Spirit and he will bind demons in my name as a result of these words of knowledge. This will bring counter attacks from The Enemy. Satan knows Jonathan's weakness. The Evil One is aware of the pain Jonathan has suffered. He is aware of the hatred that bred and multiplied in Jonathan's childhood. The devil realizes the extent of Jonathan's suffering brought on by his mother's hatred. She hated his father and she hated her son, who was the carbon copy of the man she married but who couldn't heal her wounds, or his own. She beat her husband's treasure with any object inside arm's length when the child was disobedient or made mistakes. The devil fueled her hatred each and every time she raised a hand against the child who received without effort the love she desired from her husband.

And the demons fostered and nurtured Jonathan's insecurity and feeling of unworthiness every time his mother assaulted him verbally, every time she ridiculed him in the presence of other adults. And the adversaries continued to whisper lies after Abby and the abortion. And, of course, The Accuser convinced Jonathan it was his fault that an unborn child's life was terminated. And the demons latched on to Jonathan's pain when Elizabeth, though she loved Jonathan, chose financial and emotional stability over his instability and emotional insecurity. And Jonathan's need for love, combined with his feeling of unworthiness, will come to an unmanageable despair when Jonathan loses Katherine, and all of his worldly wealth.

So when Jonathan makes strides toward coming into his ministry on earth, The Enemy will send the eternal adversary of Elijah; the one evil spirit able to caress Jonathan's weakness into an uncontrollable lust. While Jonathan participates in the work of the Holy Spirit within the church, The Adversary will send the spirit of Jezebel, whose purpose is to destroy the true prophets of God.

Jonathan is a man of great sensitivity. He is not ashamed of his vulnerability and certain women find that very attractive. The women in his prayer group will find him appealing and they will wonder why a man so compassionate and gentle has not yet found a wife. And Jezebel will show herself to him in the form of a beautiful, wounded, married woman. This woman will see everything her unbelieving husband is not in the person of Jonathan. Jezebel will spur this beautiful woman to entice Jonathan through flattery at first. Then, the woman will share with Jonathan the guilt she feels because of her past infidelity to her husband. And the seed will be planted.

Jonathan will fight against the impure thoughts each time she comes to church in her provocative skirts. He will begin to slip when he sees her breasts as she bends over in front of him to pick up her purse. He will become a willing participant in sin as she begins to share with Jonathan the sexual difficulties she and her husband are having. She will explain why she is no longer sexually attracted to her husband because he is a non-believer. She will actually share details of the marriage bed with Jonathan, all in the guise of needing prayer for her failing marriage. And Jonathan, completely enthralled by the snare, will have sex with the woman. And two more Christians, who desire freedom from bondage, will succumb to the temptation of the flesh.

The woman - unable to deal with her feelings of guilt - will explain, after the deed, that she thought she could trust him. She will explain that she believed he was a true man of God, but, in the end, he turned out to be the same as all the rest. She will tell him, as she pulls on the sexiest shorts she owns - the shorts Jonathan pulled off as she half-heartedly protested - that when given the chance alone with her, he became so full of lust that she could not stop him. And, as she buttons the see-through blouse Jonathan had taken off, she will explain that once he had become an animal with only one thought in his mind, and had proven he was determined to get what he wanted, that she just laid there and allowed him to do the deed. She will tell him that she didn't enjoy it, that she just let it happen so it would be over as soon as possible. Then she will leave. He will not even get up as she lets herself out.

And Jonathan's mind will become so numb that he will walk away from the church. He will confess his sin, and he will confess that he is not worthy of God's love. He will confess that he sickens himself and that he is the worst of all hypocrites. He will confess that he is not worthy to represent me and that everything he's ever done in my name was a lie. He will confess the hatred he has for himself and he will meander without aim or purpose for about a year. He will slowly drift through the haze of his life, but he will vacillate between good and evil. He will have been baptized in the Spirit; he will have tasted of the heavenly gift; he will have come to the living waters and experienced true life, if only for a brief moment. He will doubt himself and his calling, but he will never be rid of the knowledge that the Holy Spirit descended upon him and took up residence. He will never deny that God had spoken to him in dreams. He will vacillate. This wandering through his spiritual life – sometimes hot, sometimes cold – will go on for almost twenty years. But through all of his days, he will acknowledge a love for God. His lukewarm condition will be the result of his own feelings of guilt and unworthiness.

When he is thirty-three years old, he will travel east to the University that sits on a hill. And the University will become for him that city on the hill written about centuries ago. The dreams he receives from the Father will never leave his mind's eye, nor will they depart from his knowing place; the center of his being, the tabernacle where the Holy Spirit has taken up residence but currently remains behind the curtain that shrouds his heart. He will wander in and out of the Catholic Church he was raised in for fifteen years, until he eventually becomes lost in the world again and stops going to church altogether. But he will remember his dreams. And he will believe the lie that as long as he can still speak in tongues he has proof that God lives in him, and that as long as God lives in him his salvation is secure. He will lead a precarious existence, but the Father has chosen him, and it is not Father's desire for me to lose any he has chosen. This is why you will be sent to save him from not one, but two potentially fatal automobile accidents. Father will be left with no other devices but to bring Jonathan, once again, to the brink of despair which only finds relief in suicide. And like Elijah, when he asked Father to take his life after Jezebel made her threats against him, you will strengthen Jonathan just enough to enable him to get up and travel one more day's journey. And just as Elijah made his way to the place Father's provisions waited for him, Jonathan will find his way to Vineyard Church; the home Father has prepared for his prophet on earth. And also like Elijah, Jonathan will leave a double portion of the anointing on him to the next generation of the church, and the church will once again defeat the spirit of Jezebel, who is currently accompanied by such idols as pornography, sodomy, same-sex marriage, sexual immorality, and vanity.

Jonathan's earthly father will come home to the room I have prepared for him when Jonathan is forty-eight years old; his mother will have already been here for five years. Jonathan will operate in the gift of teaching, preaching, and prophecy, and those gifts will be used to deliver six eulogies – including both his mother's and father's – and as a teacher of Literature whose special talent is integrating Scripture and Mythology with amazing dexterity in the arena of Public Education. He will be known as an inspirational speaker and will be asked to speak at several venues in the secular world, all the while being shaped and molded by the sovereignty of The Almighty. Then, when the time has come, Father will abruptly take him out of the world and will deliver him to the church when he is fifty-two years old. Jonathan will doubt his calling as prophet and will certainly find it difficult to believe he has the spirit of Elijah upon him. He will require much convincing, because he will believe the lie that he disqualified himself because of his history of sexual immorality. The church will be cautious with him at first, which is prudent, because he will splash on them seemingly as one who fell from the sky. And when the time is right, the church will acknowledge that Jonathan's arrival is very similar to Elijah's coming on the scene all those centuries ago, which are as only a few days in the context of eternity, where time is stripped of its power. The church will acknowledge that little was known of Elijah, or where he came from, when Jehova called the Tishbite to begin his ministry on the Lord's behalf. And the Holy Spirit will illuminate Jonathan's knowing place, and give him insight into the truth that Elijah was only a man. Elijah himself was a man very far along in years before his ministry began. And, Elijah, like all men, suffered from being a sinner. Jonathan will come to realize that God does not choose men who are perfect to do his work; if that were so, none would qualify. Jonathan will learn that instead of perfection, Father looks for a heart willing to grow through which to do His work.

And Jonathan will find his treasure...he will find his GOLD. Jonathan will learn, painfully, the same truth the fictional character Herzog learned: that 'Every treasure is guarded by dragons; that's how you can tell its valuable.' *Jonathan, in learning Compassion, will be brought to his Passion. He will learn what it is he is willing to suffer for...his true vocation. And then he will be ready to become a warrior.*

It is the lover in a man who loves the one precious thing, and tells him what it is; but it is the warrior who agrees to endure the suffering the choice entails. He will learn that in agreeing to pursue the one precious thing – his true vocation – he will awaken the inner king in him that has been asleep for so many years.[14]

Paul will help Jonathan rebuild the bridge to his own greatness. As his mentor, Paul will reconnect Jonathan to his greatness and to the GOLD that was deposited in his heart when God knit him together in the womb.

Jonathan, in learning to be a gardener – and holy lover – will be required to spend three years set apart and being consecrated by the Holy Spirit. He will be forced, by the Father, to make an exit from ordinary life, because in ordinary life people attempt to satisfy their longings and fill the emptiness. But in ritual space, he will learn to experience the emptiness and longing and not fill it. Such a man can be in the presence of innocence without moving to have sexual intercourse with it.[11]

In the dream, a rider dressed in black and riding a black horse appeared on the horizon from the east – from the Holy Land. This rider brings with him financial destruction and famine, which Jonathan will experience. But the black horse also represents the sinful nature, untouched by spirit or consciousness. The black horse must come forward before his growth begins.

Jonathan's life has followed the symbolic pattern of the masculine sequence. He rode the red horse for an extended period of time, because he did not receive the father's blessing. During that time, women made love to him, and four of them seriously considered marrying him. But women will never marry such a man, because he is still unfinished. When on the red horse, he shouts at people, flares up, is fierce. Women can love such a man, but they can't trust him very far.[12]

Jonathan will come to a place, however, when he is able to endure riding the black horse. It is after the black horse appears that he will make the descent into his woundedness. When he is able to ride the black horse, the horse itself will carry him to the place his wound lives. The black horse must come before he can become GOLD.[13]

In order for Jonathan to carry out his ministry on earth, he must learn of the positive male energy that accepts authority. This authority is given, not taken by force. This positive male energy encompasses intelligence, robust health, compassionate decisiveness, good will, and generous leadership.[18] Positive male energy is authority accepted for the sake of the community. And in order to understand this golden energy, Jonathan must experience poverty.

As Jonathan travels with Paul, he will address wounds to his soul and his emotions. He will learn of poverty and he will be humbled. He will learn to trust completely in the Father. He will come to understand that shame and self-pity are tools of The Enemy, and as such, have no true power over him. And he will learn that true godliness with contentment is itself great wealth. His heart will turn to God and where his heart is, there also will his treasure be. He is in the hands of the Holy Alchemist now, and he will be tested in the crucible of fire. And he has come to the true Philosopher's Stone, which is me. And I will teach him to be proud of being my servant, which will be foolishness to the world. And as he becomes smaller and smaller in the eyes of the world, he will become larger and larger in the kingdom of God. He will be purified by the power of the Holy Spirit, and he will be transformed from base metal, which is made for ignoble purposes, into gold, which cannot be tarnished and is useful to further the Kingdom of God on earth.

Adam was banished from the Tree of Life through rejecting God's word. All who now accept and obey the word of God are brought back to the Tree of Life. To the one who is victorious, I will give the right to eat from the Tree of Life, which in in the paradise of God.[14]

The Lord has set before Jonathan a promise. The same promise he set before the Israelites in the desert. The promise His servant Ezekiel recorded in his book:

I myself will take a shoot from the very top of a cedar and plant it; I will break off a tender sprig from its top-most shoots and plant it on a high and lofty mountain. On the mountain heights of Israel I will plant it; it will produce branches <u>AND BEAR FRUIT</u> and become a splendid cedar. Birds of every kind will nest in it; they will find shelter in the shade of its branches. All the trees of the field will know that I the Lord bring down the tall tree and make the low tree grow tall. I dry up the green tree <u>AND MAKE THE DRY TREE FLOURISH</u>.[15]

I the Lord have spoken, and I will do it.

PARABLE III

The Prison

He sat in a prison cell. He was surrounded by vicious dogs all around. The dogs struck at his heels, hungry, on the verge of devouring him. In desperation, he called for the guard. The guard approached the cell, and Jonathan pleaded, "Please. I can't take it any longer." He was on the brink of hysteria as he begged the guard, "Please. I can't take it. I want to be executed."

"Once you are placed on Death Row, you cannot be taken off," said the guard.

"I don't care," the desperate man replied. "Please! I want to be executed!"

The guard acquiesced, and walked away. Within seconds, the guard returned and unlocked Jonathan's cell. The dogs remained in the cell and seemed to be submissive to the guard. "You have a phone call," the guard informed Jonathan.

"Hello," Jonathan said, as he put the phone to his ear.

"Hello, Jonathan." It was his father.

"Hello, father. I've asked them to execute me. I can't take it anymore."

"You've made a terrible mistake, Jonathan," said his father.

"It's ok, father. I just can't take it any longer."

"*You don't understand, son.* **YOU ONLY HAVE TO BE IN THERE FOR THREE YEARS, AND THEN YOU'LL BE FREE**.*"*

Jonathan hung up the phone and called for the guard again. "I didn't know that I would be free in three years," he explained. "I know I can make it for three years."

"The only one who can get you off Death Row is the warden," the guard replied.

"Please, guard. Please! Take me to the warden."

Once again, the guard acquiesced to Jonathan's wishes. He led Jonathan to the warden's office and escorted him inside. Once in the warden's office, Jonathan pled his case:

*"Please, sir," Jonathan hesitantly began. "I didn't know that I only had to be in here for three years, and then I would be free. I know I asked to be executed, sir, **but I'm not the same man I was when I came in**. Please. I'm not the same man I was."*

The warden stood up and spoke. "I believe you," the warden said. The warden studied the man. "I have compassion on you," he said. "I will take you off of Death Row."

"Thank you, sir," Jonathan said.

The guard led Jonathan back to his cell and locked the door. As the guard walked away, Jonathan noticed the dogs, who remained inside the cell with him. But now the dogs were different. They were still vicious, but they kept their distance. And Jonathan, girded up with all this new knowledge, was aware – in his knowing place – the dogs could not hurt him.

Jonathan laid in bed for several minutes. He knew God had spoken to him because of the unique quality of the dream. He'd come to recognize the difference – in his knowing place. As he shared the details of this dream with Father Thomas, the priest narrowed his eyes, studying the young man God had placed in his care for the moment. He did not take this lightly.

"The guard in your dream is the Holy Spirit. The warden is Jesus, and your father in the dream is God, the Father." Father Thomas spoke cautiously. He was not convinced after the first two dreams; but after this one, he was sure God was at work in his young friend's life.

"And the dogs?" asked the dreamer.

"The dogs represent the sins of the flesh," said Thomas. "You said that you would be free in three years?"

"That's right."

"One thing you must always remember, Jonathan. God speaks in metaphors and symbolism. Symbolism is the language of God. Three is a very important number in Scripture. It represents spiritual perfection."

"I see," Jonathan replied. "So I shouldn't try to interpret them literally?"

"Hardly ever. And you must also remember that God is speaking to *YOU* through these dreams. He is not speaking to me. In the end, you must discover the ultimate meaning on your own, through the guidance of the Holy Spirit."

Father Thomas was more than a little concerned. Frankly, he didn't think the dreams would continue, and he didn't think Jonathan would become so dependent on them. But not only had the dreams continued, they had increased in frequency. Jonathan was receiving Major Dreams, which would take years to work themselves out, but he was also beginning to receive specific dreams about specific people. Jonathan was beginning to have dreams that gave him specific knowledge into other people's lives and circumstances. This was concerning. It was a source of trepidation for the priest. Jonathan was even receiving discernment of spirits in his dreams which applied to situations in the physical world – not the real world, for anyone versed in the things of God knows that what is real are the things unseen.

Either Jonathan was involved in something very dangerous, or he really *WAS* a seer...in the biblical sense.

"Be careful, Jonathan," the priest said as Jonathan rose to leave his office. "Be careful and go with God."

It would be the last time Jonathan spoke to Thomas about his dreams. Jonathan knew the priest was apprehensive and he understood why. It would be several weeks before Jonathan felt secure enough to pursue the meaning of The Prison. And Raphael sat watching. And waiting. And The Almighty gave Raphael orders of a strange nature. He was instructed to lead Jonathan to his *Oxford Companion to the Bible*. This in itself was not so strange, but Jehova instructed Raphael to lead the dreamer to the section about Carl Jung. At first, Raphael silently wondered about his Master's plan. But after Jonathan began to read, the Lord's method came into view. Jonathan was conflicted about the method of communication The Creator had chosen with him, and he was in need of encouragement. He knew putting so much faith in dreams was treading on dangerous ground, but he also knew, in his heart, that he could distinguish his Master's voice from the voice of others. Still, he needed reassurance and he found it in the strangest of places. He learned from, of all people, the controversial scientist of dreams:

"The immediate living God who stands, omnipotent and free above His Bible and His church, who calls upon man to partake of his freedom."[1]

Even Raphael's eyes were opened. This was becoming rather fascinating even to the Healing Angel, who had certainly seen his share of fascinating marvels. And both of them read on with wonderment:

"Jung endorsed the view that 'all scripture is inspired by God and useful for teaching, for reproof, for correction, and for training in righteousness, so that everyone who belongs to God may be proficient,

equipped for every good work' (2 Timothy 3: 16). Insofar as religious statements are 'psychic confessions' deriving from the unconscious, they are like dreams that enter consciousness to inspire new insight and illumination."[2]

The dream of The Prison came to Jonathan in March of 1987. In March of 2015, Jonathan sat in a hotel room that had been converted into an apartment. This was now his home: a dilapidated hotel room with a bed, a television, a mini fridge, a microwave, a sink, a toilet, and a shower. He had lost everything he owned, save a few books, a modest wardrobe, and some articles that had sentimental value, such as a photograph of his grandparents on their wedding day, his father on the day of his First Communion, and a black-and-white photograph of Robert Kennedy, his secular hero.

On this particular night, Jonathan sat in his 12' X 20' home, wondering if the gift card his sister sent in the mail would arrive the next day. At present, he didn't have enough gas to drive to work and if the gift card didn't come, he would not eat. Luckily, he had learned to overlook affliction and keep his eyes on the Lord. He had learned through his current difficulties, of which he had already borne for a year, to *"Beware of turning to evil, which you seem to prefer to affliction."*[3] **He had also learned the reality of** *"Give me neither poverty nor riches, but give me only my daily bread. Otherwise, I may have too much and disown you and say, 'Who is the Lord?' Or I may become poor and steal, and so dishonor the name of my God."*[4] **Secure in his faith in the providence of God, he sat on the one chair he owned at the plastic self-assembled book shelf which now served as his desk, and wrote down the revelation of his dream:**

It is fourteen months now since God, our heavenly Father saved my life; stripping me of nearly all worldly possessions, the position of prestige I had achieved in the world, and the pride which comes from believing the vain flattery of those who see in a person the potential for worldly gain that comes in several forms. This is the second time that God, because of my own stubbornness and arrogance, has been forced to take from me any material value that would recommend me in the eyes of the world. The Lord shook me on a rainy and stormy night seventeen months ago, when the over-priced and stylish vehicle I was driving began to hydroplane on the interstate at seventy miles per hour. I escaped the accident, through the intervention of an angel, with my physical body intact, while my eternal soul hovered in a state of unfathomable danger. This was the second time the angel had saved my earthly life from death behind the wheel of an automobile.

As I sat alone in my fashionable apartment, listening to the storm rage outside and reliving the accident in my mind's eye, I was overwhelmed with the realization that I should have died. The car was beyond repair, a mangled and twisted mockery of what is was when it rolled off the production line. A darkness filled my soul as the truth settled in my mind: I was truly alone. Not one person who loved me was even aware of what I'd survived that night. The storm raged and my cell phone was out of service. If I had died in that accident, the closest relative was two hours away. I had, unwittingly and led by the hand of Lucifer, completely isolated myself.

This incident served to stir the spiritual complacency I had fallen into. No. The truth be known, my spiritual complacency had several years since eroded into depravity. But the incident, nonetheless, served to rouse me from a stupor. But the near-death experience had not awakened my soul completely. Lucifer's handiwork had led me to establish sturdy walls around my heart. The Almighty had no other recourse but to shake me again three months later.

My condition of isolation had become so complete that I forsook even the family I did have. I spent that Thanksgiving alone, and the Christmas holiday as well. Unawares in my intellect, the shame I felt as the fifty-year-old single man superseded my ability to understand that isolating myself ensconced me even further into the hands of Satan.

The Heavenly Father, thankfully, ripped me away from the grips of The Evil One in the only fashion he could: he stripped me of all things worldly, most of all any dignity I projected to possess. And so here I sit. Without anything to recommend me in the world's eyes, but gaining everything valuable in the Kingdom of God, which is the only true life available to human beings.

And the fire of God's Holy Spirit burns in me brighter each day as the grip of the world is loosened. I can find no rest until I write down what God the Father has spoken to me. The revelation of THE PRISON:

The dogs. Furious. Vicious. Wanting to devour me: **"My enemies surround me like a pack of dogs; an evil gang closes in on me" (Psalms 22: 16).** The dogs surrounded me. They were relentless. I sought death as relief: **"Outside the city are the dogs – the sorcerers, the sexually immoral, the murderers, the idol worshipers, and all who love to live a lie" (Revelation 22: 15).** I was in a desperate state, preferring death. But when I realized that I could be free, though I remained in the prison, the dogs could not harm me. The dogs represent desires of the sinful nature. The Holy Spirit led me to Cain:

"Then the Lord said to Cain, 'Why are you angry? Why is your face downcast? If you do what is right, will you not be accepted? But if you do not do what is right, <u>sin is crouching at your door; it desires to have you, but you must master it'"</u> (Genesis 4: 6, 7).

The sin crouching at the door of Cain, desiring to have him, was embodied in the dogs of my dream. They desired to have me. The sinful nature. But God says that sin can be mastered. In the dream, once I had the knowledge I would be free, the dogs kept their distance and could not harm me...they had been mastered. But how? How are they mastered? Through Jesus, yes, but why the prison then? What does Cain have to teach me? And the Holy Spirit showed me 1 John:

"We must not be like Cain, <u>who belonged to the evil one</u> and killed his brother. And why did he kill him? <u>Because Cain had been doing what was evil</u>" (1 John 3: 12).

Cain killing Abel was not the result of an isolated incident. Cain had been doing what was evil and he belonged to the evil one. This is why, in Genesis 4, we read that "but on Cain and his offering he (God) did not look on with favor." Because Cain already had been doing evil before he and his brother offered their sacrifices. And it is by faith that Abel brought a better sacrifice than Cain. And without faith it is impossible to please God.

And Cain represents the Law, while his brother, Abel, represents Grace. And this Grace is the result of faith. And man cannot please God through works, but only by faith in the redeeming act of Jesus on The Cross. In my case, this Divine faith took far too long to take root in my heart. And thus I was in need of Holy incarceration under the care of the Holy Spirit:

"Before the coming of this faith, we were held in custody under the law, locked up until the faith that was to come would be revealed. So the law was our guardian until Christ came that we might be justified by faith. Now that this faith has come, we are no longer under a guardian" (Galatians 3: 23-25).

What remains now is my sanctification, also under the care of the Holy Spirit. May it come to full growth soon, and may I not hinder the work of the Spirit in my weakness. May I accept the sanctifying process with the result of ever-increasing faith in our Lord Jesus Christ and belief in the sovereignty of God our Heavenly Father.

I am retracing my steps, as best I can. Steps which led to the revelation of the message delivered to me twenty-eight years ago. It has taken me this long to fully understand the message through a combination of life experiences and study of Scripture. Each time, over the better part of the past three decades, that I wanted to give up searching for the full interpretation, I was reminded of Joseph and his dreams. And each time I became faint of heart, the Spirit comforted me with the knowledge that it took Joseph the same amount of time to see his dreams come to fruition.

With partial insight into the meaning of the dogs, my search brought me to the purpose of The Prison. The Guard is the Holy Spirit. The Warden, who releases me from Death Row, is Jesus. My earthly father, who calls me, represents our Heavenly Father. I am in prison, but it is the will of the Father, who has called me, to remain in the prison for three years. And three years represents spiritual perfection. I will attempt, to the best of my ability, to explain the interpretation of The Prison as it was given to me. If it is Father's will that I remain in prison until I experience spiritual perfection, what does the prison represent?

"For this is the will of God, that you should be consecrated – separated and set apart for pure and holy living: that you should abstain and shrink from all sexual vice;" (1 Thessalonians 4: 3). If I am to be completely honest, sexual immorality has been my chief sin; the very sin that had gained mastery over me. I have defiled myself and have also defiled more than fifty women over the course of my sinful life. Of one fact I am certain: that God will not allow my union with the bride he has prepared for me until I learn **"to acquire a wife in a way that is holy and honorable, not in passionate lust like the heathen, who do not know God" (1 Thessalonians 4: 4, 5).** I was on a path which led to the eternal death of my soul. Without the intervention of God, I would have forfeited my soul in exchange for a euphoric sensation that feeds the sinful nature's appetite, but lasts only for a moment and then requires more sensation as the hunger grows over time. And the appetite is never satisfied. It is only appeased for a fleeting moment, then grows. And I can only thank God that he loved me enough to place me under incarceration. **"For God did not call us to be impure, but to live a holy life. Therefore, he who rejects this instruction does not reject man but God, who gives you his Holy Spirit" (1 Thessalonians 4: 7, 8).**

I came to understand the truth in the words of C. S. Lewis: *"We do not think God will love us because we are good, but that God will make us good because he loves us."*[5] I finally came to the place where I could accept God's discipline. Only then was I able to understand that the purpose of God's prison is for correction. It took me a long time, but I finally came to understand the truth of God's love for his children:

"In your struggle against sin, you have not yet resisted to the point of shedding your blood. And you have forgotten that word of encouragement that addresses you as sons:

'My son, do not make light of the Lord's discipline, and do not lose heart when he rebukes you, because the Lord disciplines those he loves, and he punishes everyone he accepts as a son.' (Proverbs 3: 11, 12).

Endure hardship as discipline; God is treating you as sons. For what son is not disciplined by his father? If you are not disciplined (and everyone undergoes discipline), then you are illegitimate children and not true sons" (Hebrews 12: 4-8).

I praise God that he has accepted me as his son. I praise God that he would not allow me to suffer the second death, which is eternal. I praise God that he compelled me to **"submit to the Father of our spirits and live!" (Hebrews 12: 9).** I praise God he loved me enough to put me in prison in order to secure my salvation. I praise God he loves me enough to transform me into the image of his first born Son, Jesus our Lord. I praise God.

"Our fathers disciplined us for a little while as they thought best; but God disciplines us for our good, that we may share in his holiness" (Hebrews 12: 10). The Holy Father loves me so much that he wants me to share in his holiness. My earthly father wanted me to be like him, and my Heavenly Father wants me to be like him as well. **"No discipline seems pleasant at the time, but painful. Later on, however, it produces a harvest of righteousness and peace for those who have been trained by it" (Hebrews 12: 11).** Being like the Heavenly Father requires being righteous. I praise God he is willing to train me in order to produce a harvest of righteousness and peace in me. I praise God he loves me enough to teach me how to be more like him. I praise God. I am slowly learning what our Savior taught us during his time on earth; that love is primarily expressed in obedience.

Where once I resented God for requiring me to serve the full amount of my sentence, I now thank him for loving me enough to do his holy work until I become the man he knows I can be…the man he dreamed of when he fashioned me. It is not God who prolongs my time in prison, it is my stubbornness and pettiness that keeps me in need of correction.

The prison gives us time, and it gives us perimeters. The purpose of sanctification is a manifestation of the call to individuation. I have had the prison experience forced upon me because of my insolence and disobedience caused by ignorance. I once despised my time in prison, but now I have discovered it is my time in prison that has allowed my interior life to unfold. I am becoming fertile, if you will. In God's Holy Prison, we learn of our life's work. The prison, when looked at through the lens of God's truth becomes not a space of confinement, but a sacred vessel. And the truth of God's Word takes root in the heart, and we know the truth through experience instead of hear-say:

"And we know that in all things God works for the good of those who love him, _WHO HAVE BEEN CALLED ACCORDING TO HIS PURPOSE_. For those God foreknew he also predestined to be _conformed to the likeness of his Son_, that he might be the firstborn among many brothers. _And those he predestined, he also called_; those he called, he also justified; those he justified, he also glorified" (Romans 8: 28-30).

I have come to realize that as God's son, I must learn those things which my earthly father was unable to teach me. I have come to understand that my time in sacred space (represented in the dream as a prison), is in fact a rite of passage from youth to maturity. Yes, it is so, and I have come to a place whence I am not ashamed to admit this: that in God's family I was merely a young boy in regard to my spiritual maturity, even though in the world's eyes I was considered a man of wisdom. I had need to learn these matters in isolation (from the world, not isolation from the church community), often in darkness, completely cut off from my former friends and from any reminders of my former life. At length, I shall emerge from this extended retirement a new man, prepared to take my place as a fully indoctrinated citizen of God's heavenly city, and ready to establish a new place of residence in the church community.

The rite of passage I am currently being trained by is, in fact, a passage from the profane to the sacred, from that which is fleeting and illusory to that which is real and eternal, from death to life. My holy incarceration has served as a death to my old life, because that life was not capable of developing the latent gifts within. My time in prison is, in fact, a time of discovery - through trial and conflict – of principles and ideas capable of carrying me into modes of action impossible in my former life.

This forced withdrawal, brought upon by the Holy Father, makes it possible for me to realize the calling on my life which would not have been answered if I had not been released for the time being from my social toils. And this I have learned as a certainty: this transfiguration in solitude can have no purpose, and perhaps even no meaning, except as a prelude to my entering into the social environment of the church home Father has created for me, until such a time as he calls me to my eternal abode with him. Finding my home in the church is the essence of the whole movement as well as its final cause.

I have learned, through experience, the truth expounded by God's faithful servant Richard Foster: "Every discipline (in my case, sexual purity) has its corresponding freedom...The purpose of the discipline is freedom...Our aim is the freedom, not the discipline...The moment we make the discipline (sexual purity) our central focus, we turn it into law, and lose the corresponding freedom" [6] The law brings death. And sin, finding its power in the law springs to life, bringing our death. We must learn to focus on the source of our life and our freedom: that is, the Lord Jesus Christ, for it is only by his sacrifice that we enjoy freedom from the death sin brings. I praise God. In essence, where once as I lived as a slave to sin, I am now free to NOT sin. The blood of The Cross has freed me from the power that sin holds over the sinful nature we were all born under.

Once I learned to get past my petty resentment toward God, I understood that God has no desire to destroy anyone who still remains in their sin. He neither has any desire to destroy anyone because of their sin. God is long-suffering and desires to be gracious. But those who persist in sin over a period of time are inviting the wrath of God because of their impenitence. I thank God he enlightened me to the choice I was making. I was choosing to one day incur God's wrath, and Thankfully God opened my eyes to the reality that his wrath allows no rest. The temporary discomfort I have experienced – days without food, nights without sleep, and the feeling of hopelessness – has served to show me a small glimpse of eternity under the wrath of God.

I was in prison. Placed there by the Father. The sinful nature, represented by the dogs was with me. But the dogs were submissive to The Guard, who is the Holy Spirit, given to me as protection and as a guide. The purpose of the incarceration is my sanctification. The Holy Spirit taught me why Jesus, our Lord and Savior, was led – by The Spirit – into the desert immediately after his baptism in the Jordan River. The Holy Spirit also illuminated my understanding of God's work with the Israelites – his chosen people – in the desert after he delivered them from bondage in Egypt (the world, in my case). And the Holy Spirit led me, in due time, to the book of Ezekiel:

"And I (the Lord) said to them, 'Each of you, get rid of the vile images you have set your eyes on, and do not defile yourselves with the idols of Egypt, I am the Lord your God" (Ezekiel 20: 7).

All who have been set apart by the Lord to be sanctified, who have been delivered from the bondage of the world (Egypt), must serve a period of time being cleansed of the idolatry they practiced while living in the world. And the gravest mistake any Christian can make, once they have been brought out of Egypt (the world), is convincing oneself that holding on to any of the idols they served will be acceptable. If there is any mistake more serious than this, it would be to convince oneself that no idols were worshiped during their time in the world (Egypt).

"But they rebelled against me and would not listen. <u>They did not get rid of the vile images they were obsessed with, or forsake the idols of Egypt</u>" (Ezekiel 20: 8). I was that man! I refused to put away certain idols and became obsessed. I praise God that he would not leave me in my sin. I praise God that he has, as he has the Israelites, chosen me to be one of his own.

"So I brought them out of Egypt and led them into the wilderness. There I gave them my decrees and regulations so they could <u>FIND LIFE BY KEEPING THEM</u>" (Ezekiel 20: 10, 11). Even though I was asking for eternal death by remaining in sin, the Father would not leave me to my own devices or desires. He placed me in the desert for the purpose of teaching me his decrees and his ways, so that my eternal soul might live.

"And I gave them my Sabbath days of rest as a sign between them and me. It was to remind them that I am the Lord, <u>who had set them apart to be holy</u>" (Ezekiel 20: 12). And though it took me so much longer than it should have. I finally came to understand that our Sabbath rest is found in Jesus. It is through faith in The Cross, that we are able to rest from our works and receive the free gift of God, namely, his Grace.

Slowly, and by degrees, the Holy Spirit taught me the revelation of the dogs and why they remained in the prison cell with me. And he also taught me why, after The Warden (Jesus) had granted me release from Death Row, that while the dogs (my sinful nature) remained, they had no power over me.

Just as the Spirit led our Savior into the desert to be tempted, he leads us into circumstances where temptation is permitted, that we may thereby be proved and disciplined for future work. And just as Jesus taught us to ask the Father to "lead us not into temptation," there are certain temptations I pray I never experience again when alone. Christ learned full obedience from being tempted. Christ suffered while being tempted. His temptations by Satan, which immediately followed his baptism, was necessary that he might deliver us from every temptation through his victory, and also of those conflicts he had with the enemy of mankind before he entered into his public ministry.[7]

There was a part of the wilderness which was uninhabited, but by "wild beasts" and here Christ was led, and with these beasts he was all alone, retired from the company of men; could have no assistance from any, and wholly destitute of any supply. And Christ was brought to this place to be tempted, that he might be tried before he entered his public work; that he might be in all things like unto his brethren; that he might have a heart as man, as well as power, as God, to succor them that are tempted. Which gives him his place as Warden of God's Holy Prison.[8]

We have all been called by God. And what have we been called to? We have been called to become one of his Holy Family. And anyone the Father calls, he desires to be sanctified – to be set apart and made holy – to be made into the image of his Son, Jesus, and the sanctification process is under the care of The Holy Spirit.

It was necessary, then, that Jesus be made like us, who must suffer before we can reign: both he that sanctifies – who washes men from their sins in his blood, renews them in the spirit of their minds, and consecrates them unto God; and they who are sanctified – who are renewed and dedicated to God; are all of one – of one nature, from one parent, Adam; for which cause he is not ashamed to call them – whom he thus sanctifies and saves; brethren – he reckons it no disparagement to him, though in respect of his divine nature he is infinitely above them, to acknowledge and deal with them as his brethren.[9]

"Both the one (Jesus) who makes people holy and those who are made holy are of the same family" (Hebrews 2: 11).

Jesus Christ has become our brother, that from Him we may each of us draw life, stored in Him, though having its source in God, which will make us His brethren, and God's children.[10]

While I chose to remain in sin, chose to hold on to certain idols from Egypt, I was choosing death. Thankfully, God brought me, through calamity, to the wonderful desert where salvation is gained. The same desert, spiritually speaking, our Lord traversed for forty days after his baptism and for forty years while the Israelites wandered. Jesus was with the Israelites in the desert, but God had planned for us from the beginning a better covenant; one sealed with the blood of his own Lamb, Jesus Christ. God's plan for us has always been life, not death, and he has always desired mercy, not sacrifice. And I have finally learned, through the crucible of experience, what Adam and Cain experienced, and what Tom Marshall has eloquently expressed:

"The relationship with God is what the Bible calls "LIFE." When the Bible speaks of life and death it always speaks of relationship, not existence. To be rightly related to the living God is life, to be cut off from him is death.

A person's spirit was intended to give him access to divine wisdom, to order and direct his life...wisdom in a person is always located in the heart, not in the head; in the spirit, not the mind."[11]

For that gift of the life there is more than Incarnation needed. Crucifixion is needed. The death of Death by death gives Death his death; and then, and then only, can He give us who were dead his life. The jar must be broken, though it be alabaster very precious, that through its lustrous surface there may shine softly radiant the light of the indwelling spirit; the body must be broken, that the house may be filled with the odor of the ointment. Christ dies and life escapes from Him as it were, and passes into the world.[12]

That life is a life of sonship. There is one way to know God and only one. "He that hath seen me hath seen the Father." There is one life, noble, pure, worthy of humanity, and only one: the life of trust in Christ, who is at once the object and pattern of our faith; and believing in whom we believe in the Father also.[13]

There is but one way by which we can become children of God, through the elder brother, who neither grudges the prodigal nor the ring nor the feast, but Himself has provided them both. We trust God when we have faith in Christ; and then be sure that He will give us of His own life; that He will invest us with the spirit of adoption and the standing of sons and daughters, that he will keep his hand about you, and never lose us. "Them thou hast given me, I have kept," He will say at last, pointing to us; and there we shall stand, no wanderer lost, a family in Heaven, whilst our brother presents us to His Father and ours, with the triumphant words, "Behold I and all the children whom thou hast given me."[14]

At some point during my period of sanctification, I was led to yet another Hebrew legend. And once again, Raphael whispered encouragement for me to find the truth behind the story. It was the story of Moses retrieving the bones of Joseph before the Israelites set out from their bondage in Egypt.

According to legend, the Egyptian magicians had stationed two golden dogs at Joseph's coffin, to keep watch, and they barked vehemently if anyone ventured close to it. The noise these dogs made was so loud it could be heard throughout the land, from end to end, a distance equal to forty days' journey. When Moses came near the coffin, the dogs emitted their warning sound, but he silenced them at once with the words, "Come, ye people, and behold the miracle! The real, live dogs did not bark, and these counterfeit dogs produced by magic attempt it!" What he said about real, live dogs and their refraining from barking (like in my dream) had reference to the fact that the dogs of the Egyptians did not move their tongues against any of the Children of Israel, though they had barked all the time the people were engaged in burying the bodies of their smitten first-born. As a reward God gave the Israelites the law, to cast to the dogs the flesh they themselves are forbidden to eat, for the Lord withholds due recompense from none of his creatures.

For several reasons God did not permit the Israelites to travel along the straight route to the Promised Land. The long sojourn in the wilderness was fraught with profit for the Israelites, as it is for us today, spiritually and materially. If they had reached Palestine directly after leaving Egypt, they would have devoted themselves entirely each to the cultivation of his allotted parcel of ground, AND NO TIME WOULD HAVE BEEN LEFT FOR THE STUDY OF TORAH. In the wilderness they were relieved of the necessity of providing for their daily wants, and they would give all their efforts to acquiring the law.[15]

And the Holy Spirit counseled me in the ways of God. And I learned, painfully and stubbornly at first, that man does not live by bread alone, but by every word that comes from the Father. And I learned the purpose of sanctification; the purpose of consecrating God's people, so they can absorb God's Word in their hearts before they come into possession of what God has prepared for them. And I learned that "no eye has seen, no ear has heard, no mind has conceived what God has prepared for those who love him. But God has revealed to us through his Spirit." And God's Spirit showed me the truth for us today found in Deuteronomy:

"The Lord your God will clear away these nations before you little by little; you will not be able to put an end to them quickly, for <u>the wild beasts would grow too numerous for you</u>" (Deuteronomy 7: 22). And I now understand, as I joyfully and thankfully sit in the Holy Prison Cell, that corruption is driven out of the hearts of believers little by little. The work of sanctification is carried on gradually; but at length THERE WILL BE COMPLETE VICTORY! Pride, security, and other sins that are common effects of prosperity, are enemies more dangerous than beasts of the field, and more apt to increase upon us. I have learned the value in the words "Let us never dare to think favorably of sin, never indulge it, nor allow ourselves in it."[16] And, indeed, the Spirit has taught me firsthand to "beware of turning to evil, which you seem to prefer to affliction" (Job 36: 21).

At this moment, as it sit in my 12' X 20' apartment, with the cold wind blowing in through the cracks around the doors and windows, my stomach feels the consequences of forty-eight hours without food. And I am fully confident the Lord is bringing to me a windfall of blessing. As I write these words, the Holy Spirit has led me to enlightenment concerning Job, the man of faith.

Job is imbued with the conviction, that even beyond Israel fellowship is possible with the One Living God, who has revealed himself in Israel; that he also there continually reveals himself, ordinarily in the conscience, and extraordinarily in dreams and visions; that there is also found there a longing and struggling after that redemption of which Israel has the chosen words of promise.[17] And I have new understanding of the words of Job when he says to Jehova: "Before I had only heard of you, but now I know you" (Job 42:5).

The Book of Job is the work of one of the wise men whose rendezvous was the court of Solomon.

I now appreciate God's trials, because they are designed to be a means of overcoming the evil that is external to us. I now appreciate God's chastisement, because it is designed for the overcoming of evil that is within us. There is conflict between evil and good in the world, which can result in victory to the good only so, that good proves itself in distinction from the evil, withstands the assault of evil, and destroys the evil that exists bound up with itself: only so, that the good as far as it is still mixed with the evil is refined as by fire, and more and more freed from it.[18]

There is a twofold point of view from which the suffering of Job is to be regarded. It was designed, first of all, that Job should prove himself in opposition to Satan, in order to overcome him: and since Job does not pass through the trial entirely without sinning, it has the effect at the same time of purifying and perfecting him.

Job serves as an example of God's sovereignty. Both Old and New Testaments agree that Satan is God's adversary, and consequently altogether evil, and must notwithstanding serve God, since God makes even evil minister to His purpose of salvation, and the working out of His plan in the government of the world.[19]

I, like Elijah and Job, though I would never be in such a state of delusion to place myself on the same plane as the two aforementioned heroes of faith, have learned from the sin of desiring death before the completion of God's plan. If a man, on account of his sufferings, wishes to die early, or not to have been born at all, he has lost his confidence that God, even in the severest suffering, designs his highest good; and this want of confidence is sin.[20]

125

The final teaching of the Book of Job is not that God's rule demands faith before everything else; the final teaching is, that sufferings are for the righteous person the way to glory, and that his faith is the way to sight.

After all that was sinful in Job's speeches - and in Elijah's speeches, and someday my own - is blotted out by repentance, there remains only the truth of our innocence, which God himself testifies to, and the truth of our holding fast to God in the hot battle of temptation, by which, without his knowing it, God has frustrated the design of Satan.

And the servant of Jehova is not only favored himself, but he also becomes the instrument of grace to sinners. As where his faith shone forth he became the prophet of his own and the friends' future, so now he is the priestly mediator between the friends and God. And it will forever remain true that a prophet's duty is to stand in the gap and intercede for those the Lord has placed in the prophet's community.[21]

***

In the end, after all intellectual discourse and scrutiny, the crux of it all comes to a simple decision to be made. We either believe God's Word is true or we don't. And if we believe it is, then all of it is true. God will require us to put faith in the entirety of His word, as he also requires his true disciples to trust in Him entirely. We must accept all of God's truth, especially those parts which bring us discomfort. Do we truly want to be recommended? Favored? Set apart? It takes more than belief in that portion of God's Word which is convenient or most tolerable or most in agreement with our own wishes.

Man cannot stand in the presence of God. His nature is wrong. Man is lost, not because of what he does, but because of what he is. We need life from God, because we are spiritually dead. Thanks be to God, Christ has redeemed us from spiritual death.[22]

The new man, Jesus Christ, had no death in him. He was not born as we were born, and he didn't have the spiritual nature of death - the sinful nature – in him. Yet the Bible says in Hebrews 2: 9 that he tasted death for every man.

We must strive after the realization Brother Lawrence finally experienced. When he had failed in his duty, he only confessed his fault, saying to God, "I shall never do otherwise if you leave me to myself; it is you who must hinder my falling and mend what is aimless." After this he gave himself no further uneasiness about it.[23]

Brother Lawrence learned the secret things of God, and in regard to our being made holy he learned that "our sanctification does not depend on changing our works, but in doing that for God's sake which we commonly do for our own." And, finally, and with completeness, he came to understand "the greater perfection a soul aspires after, the more dependent it is upon Divine Grace."[24]

Indeed, Brother Lawrence, our great intercessor before God, who moved God's mighty hand on the Church's behalf, suffered much and for a long period of time. He himself says, "I must tell you that for the first ten years I suffered much. The apprehension that I was not devoted to God as I wished to be, my past sins always present to my mind, and the great unmerited favor which God did me, were the matter and source of my sufferings."[25]

And the man who stood in the gap between the church and God very effectively suffered through periods of deep darkness. "When I thought of nothing but to end my days in these troubles (which did not at all diminish the trust I had in God, and which served only to increase my faith), I found myself changed all at once; and my soul, which until that time was in trouble, felt a profound inward peace, as if she were in her center and place of rest."[26]

So what solace can we take from Brother's experience? At the very least this: "We know that we can do all things with the Grace of God, which he never refuses to them who ask it earnestly. Knock, persevere in knocking, and I answer for it that He will open to you in His due time, and grant you all at once what He has deferred during many years."[27]

God is Love and Happiness is a choice. Choose to seek God and know that He is within us and we need not seek Him elsewhere.

And we can know God's heart toward us who were once estranged and unfaithful by looking at his prophet Hosea. The name *Hosea* means *Salvation*. God, the grieved lover desires to win back His love. He took Israel (and us) to the solitary wilderness, where she could hear His voice without distraction.

Vineyards, which speak of prosperity and fruit-bearing, would be given by God to His restored people (and us). Only through Achor (trouble), could Israel (and us) come back to fellowship with the Lord and its resultant blessing.[28]

And anyone who truly desires to be made into the image of God's Son, must come to terms with the truth that the process requires us being put to many tests throughout our lives. The Psalmist speaks truth in 105:19, saying, "Until the time that His Word came to pass, the Word of the Lord tried him."

There is a "dark night of the soul" for some of God's true children; a prolonged and painful period when God seems to be altogether absent, when days are dark and nights are long, when tomorrow holds no promise of light or alleviation from Hopelessness, when the rest of the grave is preferred to the wearisome round of suffering and sorrow.[29]

But anyone who desires to be made a noble vessel for God's purpose, must know that delay never thwarts God's purpose; rather, it polishes his instrument. You were called to be free. But do not use your freedom to indulge the flesh; rather serve one another humbly in love. If you bite and devour each other (like vicious dogs), watch out or you will be destroyed by each other.

The acts of the flesh are many, the first of them being sexual immorality, which opens the door for a plethora to follow. Idolatry, hatred, jealousy, fits of rage, selfish ambition, dissensions, factions, envy, drunkenness; those who live like this will not inherit the Kingdom of God.[30]

And Scripture pictures all mankind as sinners shut up and imprisoned by sin, so that the inheritance which was promised through faith in Jesus Christ, the Messiah, might be given to all those who believe – who adhere to and trust in and rely on Jesus. And before the faith came we were perpetually guarded under the law, kept in custody in preparation for the faith that was destined to be revealed.

But now that faith has come, we are no longer under a trainer – the Guard. For in Christ Jesus we are all children of God through faith. This is a trustworthy analogy: as long as the heirs (us) are spiritually incomplete, we are no different from slaves, although we are the masters of all the estate; but we are under guardians and administrators or trustees until the date fixed by the Father (three years, in my case). So we also, while we are still immature spiritually, are kept like slaves under the elementary teachings of a system of external observations and regulations, namely, the law. And the sole purpose of the law is to make us aware of our sinfulness. [31]

And thankfully, in Jesus we were circumcised with a circumcision not performed by human hands. Your whole self, ruled by the flesh, was put off when you were circumcised by Christ, having been buried with him in baptism, in which you were also raised with him through your faith in the working of God, who raised Jesus from the dead. [32] This is God's word. It is either true or it is not. If it is true, we need only to believe it.

And Jesus said that if we hold to His teaching, we are really His disciples. Then we will know the truth, and the truth will set us free. When we were dead in our sins and in the uncircumcised condition of our sinful nature, God made us alive with Christ. He forgave us all our sins, having cancelled the written code, with its regulations, that was against us and stood opposed to us; He took it away, nailing it to The Cross. [33] This is either true or it is not.

The Jews are God's chosen people, and so are we, for a true Jew is one whose heart is right with God. And true circumcision is not merely obeying the letter of the law; rather, it is a change of heart produced by

129

the Spirit. For no one can ever be made right with God by doing what the law commands. The law simply shows us how sinful we are. Yet God freely and graciously declares that we are righteous. He did this through Christ Jesus when He freed us from the penalty of our sins. We cannot boast, then, that we have done anything to be accepted by God, because our acquittal is not based on obeying the law. It is based on faith. But, just because we emphasize faith, this does not gives us leave to forget about the law. In fact, only when we have faith do we truly fulfill the law. And Jesus did not come to abolish the law, but to fulfill it.[34]

Clearly, God accepted Abraham before he was circumcised. The circumcision was only a sign that Abraham already had faith and that God had already accepted him and declared him to be righteous – even before he was circumcised.

Clearly, God's promise to give the whole earth to Abraham and his descendants was based not on his obedience to God's law, but on a right relationship with God that comes by faith. For the law always brings punishment on those who try to obey it. But we died to the law through the body of Christ, so we might belong to God, in order that we might bear fruit. Once we were controlled by the sinful nature, the sinful passions aroused by the law were at work in our bodies, and we bore fruit for death. We were once slaves to sin, which results in spiritual death. But now, by dying to what once bound us, we have been released from the law so that we serve in the new way of the Spirit, and not in the old way of the written code.[35]

If God's Word is true, then our sinful selves were crucified with Christ so that sin would lose its power in our lives. Once we were slaves to sin, because of our sinful nature. But no more! When we died with Christ during baptism, we were set free from the power of sin. This is either true or it is not. We now can choose not to let sin control the way we live; we have the choice not to give in to sinful desires. Sin is no longer our master, because we no longer live under the requirements of the law. Instead, we live under the freedom of Grace. I choose to believe the truth that we are free from the power of sin, and lo, freedom is at hand!

We have a choice! And we become slaves to whatever we choose to obey. We can be slaves to sin, which leads to death, or we can choose to obey God, which leads to righteous living. Now I am free from slavery to sin, and I have become a slave to righteous living.[36] Thank God!

I have learned the truth. The dogs, the sinful nature, had me fooled. But now I know the truth. They have no real power over me. I am no longer fooled! Previously, I allowed myself to be a slave to impurity and lawlessness, which led even deeper into sin. But now I have been afforded the opportunity to give myself over to being a slave to righteous living so that I will become holy, as God intends.

When I was a slave to sin, I was free from the obligation to do right. And the end result was being ashamed of the things I once did – things that lead to eternal doom. But now I am free from the power of sin and have become a prisoner of God. And, thanks be to God, I now do those things that lead to holiness and result in eternal life. The wages of sin is death, but the free, the free...it's free – the free gift of God is eternal life through Christ Jesus our Lord.[37]

And I have begun to see how truly evil Satan is; him and his dogs. I have discovered that the law's commands, which were supposed to bring life, brought spiritual death instead. Sin – the dogs – took advantage of those commands and deceived me; the dogs used the commands to kill me, to bring about the death of my eternal soul. Sin – the dogs – used the law, which is good, to bring about my condemnation to death. I now see how terrible sin really is. It uses God's commands for its own evil purposes.[38] And now, I truly despise the sin I once enjoyed. I hate it for the false promises it made; I hate it for trying to take me down to hell; I hate it for hating me; and I hate it for being against my Father, who loves me; and I hate it for causing our beautiful Savior to suffer on The Cross. But it is sin who loses in the end, because The Savior lives forever and sin suffers for eternity. But sin will not suffer with me; sin's misery will not have my company.

The dogs have lost their power over me. Day after day, I am being sanctified by the Holy Spirit. Day after day, I am learning how to live by the Spirit. Once I inevitably did what was wrong, even though I love God's law with all my heart. I agree with God's commands in my mind as well. But there is another power within me that is at war with my mind. This power once made me a prisoner of sin. I was once miserable, unable to see how I could be free from this life that is dominated by sin and death. But the truth has set me free! If God's Word is true, THERE IS NO CONDEMNATION FOR THOSE WHO BELONG TO CHRIST JESUS. And because I belong to Him, the power of the life-giving Spirit has freed me from the power of sin – the dogs – that leads to death.[39]

I was once dominated by the dogs – sin – and thought about sinful things. But now I am a prisoner of the Spirit and I choose to think about things that please the Spirit. I have the power to choose! Once I allowed the sinful nature to control my mind, which leads to death. But now I choose to be a prisoner of the Holy Spirit and think about that which pleases Him, which leads to life and peace.[40]

God's Word is either true or it is not. And God has told us that everyone who believes that Jesus is the Christ has become a child of God. And every child of God defeats this evil world, and we achieve this victory through our faith. And this is also what God has testified: He has given us eternal life, and this life is in His Son. Whoever has the Son has life; whoever does not have God's Son does not have life. And we know that God's children do not make a practice of sinning, for God's Son holds us securely, and the evil one – much less his dogs – cannot touch us.[41]

There now remains only one measuring line, and that standard is love. For anyone who loves is a child of God and knows God. But anyone who does not love does not know God, for God is love. We love each other because God loved us first. If we love our brothers and sisters who are believers, it proves that we have passed from death to life. But a person who has no love is still dead.[42] So I shall test myself daily. I will pursue patience and kindness; I shall remain hopeful and endure every circumstance; I will be polite and forgiving, keeping no record of wrongs; I will pursue honesty and justice; I will be faithful and determined to persevere, because I have learned that success is in getting up one more time than I fall. I will not be jealous or boastful; I will not be proud or demand my own way; I will not be irritable or vindictive, for I have a power not even afforded to the angels – I have the power to choose.[43]

And I choose to believe, nay, I now have knowledge in my heart – my knowing place – that what Paul wrote to the Thessalonians is true:

"May God himself, the God of peace, _SANCTIFY YOU THROUGH AND THROUGH_. May your whole spirit, soul and body be kept blameless at the coming of our Lord Jesus Christ. _THE ONE WHO CALLS YOU IS FAITHFUL AND HE WILL DO IT._"[44]

Can you believe it? Do we dare believe it? The God of Peace will "sanctify you through and through." Can it really be this easy? Can we really understand the meaning of Divine Love and believe that "The one who calls you is faithful and HE will do it." Oh how unfathomable and unmeasurable the depth of God's love for us.

So, this truth is mine. God has spoken it and it is true. God spoke the world into existence and God spoke these words into my life. God has declared: "Your covenant with death will be annulled; your agreement with the grave will not stand" (Isaiah 28: 18). Amen. It shall be so.

PARABLE IV

Jezebel

He was standing in the street. It was late night and the streets were empty. Suddenly, a beautiful young woman stood on the corner. She was wearing a see-through night gown, cut very short, and nothing else. Jonathan's lust was immediately awakened.

"Don't you want to touch me?" she asked.

"Yes, I do," Jonathan said. "But you belong to the leader of the dogs."

"It's ok," she replied. She smiled, very invitingly, which pierced Jonathan's guts. "It's ok," she said again, "I want you to touch me." She came closer and touched her own breast. "Touch me," she said.

Jonathan touched her breast. He could not resist. As soon as he touched her, she stepped back, looked in the distance, and said, "Did you see that?"

Suddenly, the dogs surrounded him, just like they did in the prison. They were vicious. Hungry. All at once, the leader of the dogs came forth. The animal's red coat of fur glistened under the light of the moon. He was much larger – and fiercer – than any of the other dogs. At one point, at the height of Jonathan's fear, the leader stood still, stuck out his chest, and let out a blood-chilling cry; just to show Jonathan his power.

"But she wanted me to," Jonathan pleaded.

"That doesn't matter," the woman said, with a smirk of betrayal.

The leader of the dogs summoned another whelp from his bowels and led the charge to devour Jonathan. He ran. He saw a house. The house was surrounded by a brick wall, about eight feet tall. As the dogs gained ground on Jonathan, he saw a wooden gate in the wall. He reached the gate and saw a man behind it. The man was a stranger. The dogs advanced. In terror and desperation Jonathan opened the gate, and without thinking he instinctively grabbed the man standing there and threw him outside.

Jonathan could hear the dogs devour the man he'd thrown outside the wall as he climbed to the roof of the house. Once on the roof, the dogs, the man, and the woman were gone. Only Jonathan remained, standing on the roof of the house.

It was now twenty-eight years since Jonathan received this dream, and after the events of the past week, he knew – in his knowing place – that his break-through, and his freedom, was imminent. He didn't need to share the details of the dream with anyone. He'd lived out, and subsequently discovered the meaning himself. As Jonathan knelt in prayer, basking in the glow of the Heavenly Father's providence and love, Lucifer called a meeting with Asmodeus, Lilith, and Jezebel. Beelzebub himself had escorted the three demons to Lucifer's office:

Lucifer:	Wait outside, Beelzebub. Let none enter whilst the door is closed.
Beelzebub:	Yes, m'lord.
Lucifer:	Sit, all of you. We have a situation. Recently, a very bright light appeared on the Chief Astrologer's chart. Its brightness is at a disturbing level.
Asmodeus:	from whence dost the light shine, prince?
Lucifer:	Be silent, fiend! The Chief Astrologer has shown me the coordinates. It shines from the Midwestern area of the United States. The light belongs to Jonathan, a no-body who grew up

in western Kansas, but moved to that bastion of HIS servants in the center of America twenty years hence.

Jezebel: I remember him well, m'lord. His light was barely flickering just three years past. That light was all but snuffed out, sire.

Lucifer: Quiet, strumpet! That light, which you say was all but snuffed out, burns with the same brightness of a holy prophet now! I had Beelzebub pull his file. This is quite disturbing. Our ineptitude is unfathomable at times! When he was but two years old, I sent Asmodeus to investigate what reason HE would have sending Raphael to western Kansas. Asmodeus reported that Raphael saved this wretched boy from drowning. We should have known HE was scheming something when we noticed Raphael taking such an interest in the boy after that.

Lilith: I remember the boy now, m'lord. You sent me to pay him a visit shortly after the event you speak of. He was in the hospital, suffering from pneumonia...a rather serious case. But I was prevented entry into his room by that arrogant archangel.

Lucifer: Why did you not bring this to my attention? A gross oversight, wench!

Lilith: He was so young. And it was western Kansas. Please forgive me, sire.

Lucifer: You have me confused with HIM now. Forgiveness will never be extended here. Accountability; that is what this empire is built on. According to the file, the boy received his first dream from HIM at the age of six. The boy didn't realize he had been visited by an angel that night, so the entry level minion we sent that morning saw no reason for alarm. Blasted! No reason for alarm! Being visited by Divine Messengers at six-years-old is not cause for alarm? Someone will pay for this.

Asmodeus: What was the nature of the message, prince?

Lucifer: Not your concern! You've always been a curious fiend. I grow tired of you.

Asmodeus: Yes, prince.

Lucifer: According to the file, the boy watched his father rape the unfaithful wife when he was eight years old. His mother beat him often; more often than she beat the other children, because he was favored by the father. The wretched boy was twelve when his mother forced him to take his pants off in front of her after he complained of pain during urination. That same year, his cousin, two years older and much stronger than he, sodomized him. Tell me, demons, what do you surmise so far?

Asmodeus: It seems to me, prince, he will go the way of millions like him. He will go the way of delinquency and addiction. He appears to be no threat as far as I can see, prince.

Lucifer: And therein lies your stupidity! Most people in his position do go the way of delinquency and addiction, I grant you that. But, most people in his position are not watched over by Raphael himself! Most people in his position are not visited with a Divine Message at the age of six! HE is a wily adversary. We have allowed ourselves to become complacent with Jonathan! We were far too overconfident with this case. We shall see if it has gone so far that we cannot salvage the case yet. But one truth is evident at the moment: where the light was nearly snuffed out, it now shines with bright luster.

Jezebel: I remember having huge success with the boy when he was seventeen, sire. You assigned him to me then, and I presented him with the most beautiful maiden. She was one year younger than he. She was dark-skinned, with big brown enchanting eyes. And she had been admiring him from afar for several months. She would have done anything to keep him. It was the perfect match; she was very taken with him, and he could not resist her beauty. Once he'd experienced the thrill of being one with her in the flesh, he was putty in her hands...and mine.

Lucifer: And eventually she became pregnant.

Jezebel: Yes, m'lord. And Jonathan wanted to marry her. But I thwarted that union. I incited her father to steal her away one night. He took her three hours away to an abortion clinic and ended the life of Jonathan's unborn son. It wreaked havoc on the whole affair. It wreaked havoc with Jonathan's mental health as well. It looked as though he would break under the weight of it, but that contemptuous angel kept showing up at the most inopportune moments.

Lucifer: Enough babbling on! The abortion was performed in April of the year 1979 on the human calendar. Let us move ahead to December 24ᵗʰ of 1986. The night he received the first dream from HIM as an adult. His light began to burn much brighter after that nocturnal visitation.

Asmodeus: Ay, prince. But soon we were able to bombard the poor fool with wayward women of every type. I introduced him to pornography and Lilith became active with the wretch as well.

Lilith: He speaks the truth, sire. He was soon addicted to auto-erotic gratification, thanks to my nocturnal visits.

Jezebel: But then he found support in a church for a time, and his light burned brighter than ever. That's when you assigned me to his case indefinitely, sire.

Lucifer: I have not need for you to inform me of my own actions, whore! I was there, watching — albeit from quite a distance — when the minister prophesied over the young man. The spirit of Elijah upon him! I saw it, that blueish glaze surrounding him as the minister spoke. And then I assigned you to his case indefinitely. And you were given specific instructions: Do not allow this one to find his calling.

Jezebel: Indeed, m'lord. And soon thereafter I presented myself to him in the form of a beautiful Christian woman whose husband was an unbeliever. He fell prey to every trick I employed. And when the infidelity had finally been achieved, he retreated with his head down, quite defeated. Since that time, his light grew fainter and fainter each time I checked it on my rounds.

Lucifer:	And look at it now! It shines brighter than ever before. I shall get to the bottom of this. Someone will pay. I shall have my vengeance! Sit, strumpet. Explain to me what has transpired in the last fifteen years. Withhold nothing. Tell all!
Jezebel:	He meandered somewhat aimlessly most of the time, sire. He would have moments of inspiration toward the light, but he always succumbed to the women I placed in his path. Married women found him quite desirable, and he has never been able to resist the forward advances of a beautiful woman who desires him.
Lucifer:	What are his talents?
Jezebel:	He's quite gifted as a teacher. Very inspirational. I have used this against him more than once. It's quite easy to ignite lust in a damsel listening to him speak.
Lucifer:	Asmodeus. Listening to this lump of vanity, one would surmise the lad has no hope of being used mightily by HIM. What can you add, or do I have to look it up for myself?
Asmodeus:	Raphael has been dispatched to help the human on several occasions. There must be something up that scoundrel's sleeve.
Lucifer:	Blasted! If Raphael is involved, something is in the mix. Let me look at his file...It says here, Asmodeus, that you had the man on the verge of suicide twice.
Asmodeus:	Indeed, sire. He lost all of his wealth and his fiancé inside of forty days once. The woman was quite handsome; a prototypical fair-skinned maiden if ever there was. And Jonathan had risen to an impressive status among men by the time he'd reached his twenty-seventh birthday. When it all collapsed, because of his pride, He found himself one night caressing the cold steel of a handgun. I kept whispering, "Do it! Do it! Ease your pain. Make the pain go away."
Lucifer:	And?

Asmodeus:	That busy-body Raphael, he swept in and caused the suffering boy to fall into a deep sleep. And then he stood guard over the boy for days at a time. He truly is a nuisance, sire.
Lucifer:	Enough! The incident you speak of took place twenty-six years ago. He had a second brush with suicide not more than fourteen months past. And in the space of those fourteen short months, his light has gone from barely a flicker to blazing white-hot and increasing in splendor. It's an outrage! How can we be so incompetent! Explain it!
Asmodeus:	It seems to me...
Lucifer:	Not you, vermin! In fact, Asmodeus, you are excused. My complaint is with these two at the moment.
Asmodeus:	Ay, m'lord.
Lucifer:	Now...we shall find the bottom of this, wenches. I'll have my satisfaction before you leave.
Jezebel:	It all began to turn, sire, when he found that disgusting church. He's found a home there, m'lord.
Lucifer:	A Vineyard. In the heart of America! This will not do! We shan't lose him now! We've got too much invested in the wretch.
Jezebel:	But he's found one who's invested more than we, sire.
Lucifer:	Do not speak of HIS SON if you know what's good for you, bitch. We need only examine the case to discover what can be done. It can't be too late to snuff out his light.
Lilith:	If I may, sire, it seems to me we have no other option but to devise a plan to sabotage the Scripture he reads.
Lucifer:	What say you? Explain your meaning.
Lilith:	Well, sire, the ploys of Jezebel and myself no longer have the same effect. He's been cloistered by HIM, and Jonathan has willingly accepted the discipline. It's as though his eyes have been opened anew as he reads from that book now. And...well...
Lucifer:	Tell all, whore. You'll not suffer my wrath. It was not you put in charge of the wretch. Tell me all. Withhold no detail.

Lilith:	Ay, m'lord. It was about three weeks ago now. I came to the run-down dump he currently lives in during my evening rounds. My aim was the same as always. The method is tried and true since days of old. I crept in and spied him sleeping in his bed. The covers were pulled up around his chin. I crawled on his bed, as always, and prepared to dispense my nocturnal visions. These visions never fail to rouse a man to auto-erotic gratification.
Lucifer:	Get to the point!
Lilith:	Well, sire, I went to pull the covers down from his ear. I was subtle as ever. And as I was poised to transmit the visions...
Lucifer:	Reveal the truth! Immediately!
Lilith:	He saw me, sire. It startled him and he sat up in his bed. He saw me. And he used that NAME to cast me out.
Lucifer:	He's been given discernment of spirits. He's coming into his calling. Why wasn't I made aware of this before now?
Jezebel:	I've cleared off my calendar since that night, sire. I've set my entire focus on him alone until our agenda is carried out.
Lucifer:	And you are failing! You are losing the battle! If you value your position the least bit, you will produce the verses he's been reading. I want them all, chapter and verse. We'll lose him for certain if we aren't familiar with the arsenal he possesses.
Jezebel:	I have them here, m'lord. I've got chapter and verse, accompanied with dates and apparent effect each verse has had on him.
Lucifer:	Make your presentation. Withhold nothing, or you'll pay dearly.
Jezebel:	As we've already spoken, he was cloistered by HIM fourteen months ago, and he willingly accepted the discipline. He went to the Book of Romans straightaway. It was at this point that another minister prophesied over him the same message that was given twenty-five years ago.
Lucifer:	So once again, twenty-five years later, and from a different minister, he received the same word from HIS SPIRIT?
Jezebel:	Ay, m'lord. That the spirit of Elijah was upon him and that I was against him. He was told that he must learn how to defeat me.

Lucifer: And you didn't think to bring this information to me?

Jezebel: I took it as a challenge, sire. I saw it as a way to prove my value to you once again. I truly thought he would go the way of so many would-be prophets who preceded him. And he was so constricted by his need for approval and affection. He was still susceptible to the advances of a beautiful woman. I still think he's doomed to fail, sire. His flesh is so habituated to the sin of sexual immorality.

Lucifer: But something has happened! There's been some kind of major break-through. Give me the verses and his reactions to them.

Jezebel: It seems the most important breakthrough for him came just four months ago. He was reading from the sixth chapter of Romans:

"...don't you know that all of us who were baptized into Christ Jesus were baptized into his death? We were therefore buried with him through baptism into death in order that, just as Christ was raised from the dead through the glory of the Father, we too may live a new life" (Romans 6: 3, 4).

Lucifer: But he was baptized as an infant. He was not even aware of the benefits of baptism as an infant.

Jezebel: He was baptized again in that church he's found. Totally submerged, sire. Just four months ago. He was strengthened much by the following passage from the same book:

"...For we know that our old self was crucified with him so that the body of sin might be done away with, that we should no longer be slaves to sin – because anyone who has died has been freed from sin" (Romans 6: 6, 7).

Lucifer: But he's read that book many times before. And we've always been able to steal the power of the words away from him through sexual immorality and his subsequent feelings of guilt over his sins.

Jezebel: Truly, sire. But he no longer responds to the normal temptations. I presented myself to him in the form of a very attractive woman who professes to be Christian, but whose flesh is completely under my control.

Lucifer: With what result?

Jezebel: He stood up under the temptation, m'lord. He has an entirely new resolve. He's changed, sire. Since being cloistered, he now believes what he reads in that book and he has newfound power to put the words into practice. And he also puts into practice other books he reads, written by successful servants of HIS.

Lucifer: Give an example.

Jezebel: He employs these words often: *"Let those that think they stand, take heed lest they fall. Sin appears fair, but is vile; it appears pleasant, but is destructive, it promises much, but performs nothing. The deceitfulness of sin hardens the soul; one sin allowed makes way for another; and every act of sin confirms the habit."*

Lucifer: HIS SPIRIT has gone to work in the boy. The pitiful wretch has yielded to HIS SPIRIT. This shall not pass. Give me all the verses he's read since his baptism.

Jezebel: I've got it all here, sire. Still in the book of Romans:

"...But if Christ is in you, your body is dead because of sin, yet your spirit is alive because of righteousness. And if the Spirit of him who raised Jesus from the dead is living in you, he who raised Christ from the dead will also give life to your mortal bodies through his Spirit, who lives in you" (Romans 8: 10, 11).

Lucifer: And reading these verses now has effect in the walking out of his daily life? And he is yielding more and more to HIS SPIRIT?

Jezebel: Yes, m'lord. He believes the verses now and they have power in his life.

Lucifer: And have you exhausted all the tried and true temptations with him?

Jezebel: The opportunity rarely presents itself any longer. He's protected most of the time in his cloister. There's a hedge around him most of the time. He keeps a distance between himself and wayward women now. He can detect their waywardness, which he's been able to do in the past, but now he has a whole new sense of value as HIS son. When adversity besets him these days, instead of seeking comfort in the arms of a woman — one of my women — he runs to his cloister and, like a little child, he cries out, "I'm your son. You will not forsake me. I put my trust in you." He's become a pathetic coward, actually. Always running to hide behind HIS coat tails.

Lucifer: You must give me the rest of the verses. I must know what he knows. He's lost to us unless I know everything he knows.

Jezebel: This particular passage has been a road block to me. He actually believes it now:

> **"Therefore, brothers, we have an obligation – but it is not to the sinful nature, to live according to it. For if you live according to the sinful nature, you will die; but if by the Spirit you put to death the misdeeds of the body, you will live, because those who are led by the Spirit of God are sons of God" (Romans 8: 12, 13).**

Lucifer: He's learned the one thing we needed to keep him blind to. He's learned not to depend on his own strength. He's learned to depend on HIS SPIRIT.

Jezebel: His defenses against my ploys strengthened even deeper after reading this from the second Letter to the Corinthians:

"...if anyone is in Christ, he is a new creation; the old has gone, the new has come! All this is from God, who reconciled us to himself through Christ and gave us the ministry of reconciliation: that God was reconciling the world to himself in Christ, not counting men's sins against them" (2 Corinthians 5: 17-19).

Lucifer: *And you tempted him soon after his joy from this verse subsided?*

Jezebel: Yes, sire. Like always. But he runs from the temptation of a provocative woman now. And he refuses to watch pornography also. And he runs for HIS protection when I tempt him with visions that heretofore would have beat on him and persisted in pummeling him until he succumbed to auto-erotic gratification. He indulges himself in this practice seldom now, and even when he does, he quickly confesses the sin and then goes about his day, undaunted. It's a state of being quite new for this one.

Lucifer: *Tell me, has he learned this verse?*

"Brothers, I do not consider myself yet to have taken hold of it. But one thing I do: Forgetting what is behind and straining toward what is ahead, I press on toward the goal to win the prize for which God has called me heavenward in Christ Jesus."

Jezebel: Let me check my notes, sire.

Lucifer: *It's Philippians 3: 13, 14.*

Jezebel: Yes, sire. Here it is. Right here.

Lucifer: *He's learned that his transformation is a process. He's discovered that it can happen if he's patient and willing to stay the course.*

This is going to take drastic measures now. Tell me what else he's learned.

Jezebel: If you ask me, he's become nothing more than a coward. He rarely attempts to fight me off by his own strength, like a man. Instead, he leans on verses like this:

"...I have been crucified with Christ and I no longer live, but Christ lives in me. The life I live in the body, I live by faith in the Son of God, who loved me and gave himself for me. I do not set aside the grace of God, for if righteousness could be gained through the law, Christ died for nothing" (Galatians 2: 20, 21).

Lucifer: We would have been better off with this one if he'd become a priest all those years ago, like he wanted to for a time. Now that he's been completely stripped of his desire to perform works in order to curry favor with HIM, we've got an uphill battle ahead. What else did he learn from this particular Letter of that putrid little urchin Paul, who once showed promise for our side?

Jezebel: He sat up one night repeating this verse over and over:

"Those who belong to Christ Jesus have crucified the sinful nature with its passions and desires" (Galatians 5: 24).

Lucifer: I was afraid of that.

Jezebel: If I may, sire, something has significantly changed inside the fool. Once, not so long ago, he would say a verse like the one just mentioned and it would take little effort to persuade him that the words didn't really apply to him. It didn't take much effort to distract him away from reciting verses like these.

Lucifer: You are the fool, not him! Have I taught you nothing? You have the focus of a child sometimes! He's been given the gift of faith, you idiot. He's been given the opportunity to believe the words are true. He's been given faith!

Jezebel: It's because he's submitted to being cloistered, sire. He's submitting to HIS authority. He keeps saying, "Your will be done." It's sickening. And there's little opportunity to attack him with a covert plan, much less a frontal assault. And he took a huge step away from us when he got his hands on that book spawned by that pig Tom Marshall. He's found power against one of our most effective strategies: inner strife. He found a dangerous level of freedom with that book. Here's an example of what he wrote down in his study of the farce:

> "His mind pulls him one way, his feelings another. His bodily appetites seek satisfaction, his conscience condemns – the result is unbearable inner strife. We...

Lucifer: Enough! I'm beginning to see what we're up against. He's found the power of being transformed by the renewing of his mind. Look in your notes, dog, and see if he's put his faith in what the humans call the fourth chapter of Ephesians.

Jezebel: Yes, m'lord...yes, here it is. Ephesians 4: 22-24:

> **"You were taught, with regard to your former way of life, to put off your old self, which is being corrupted by its deceitful desires; to be made new in the attitude of your minds; and to put on the new self, created to be like God in true righteousness and holiness."**

Lucifer: You poor toad. You don't even realize what's happened. Has he been reciting this passage consistently?

Jezebel: Yes. But...

Lucifer: Enough! I am going to give a synopsis of Jonathan's journey on earth. And when I get to the present point in time, you are going to see that you're of no value to me now in regard to this one's case.

He was born to alcoholic parents. He watched his father rape his mother because of her own unfaithfulness. He watched his mother stab his father repeatedly until his father passed out in a pool of blood on the living room floor. His mother touched him in an inappropriate way after he'd complained of pain during urination. And all of this happened before his thirteenth birthday. And His cousin, two years older than he, sodomized him just weeks before he turned thirteen.

This boy had little hope for any semblance of a normal life. But HE showed favor toward the boy and sent him a dream when the boy was only six years old — very uncommon, which alerted us to the boy's potential as an ambassador of light. And even before that, HE sent Raphael to save the boy from drowning when he was only two years old. Eventually, Raphael was assigned to watch over the pathetic slime. But we were alert to what could become of the case.

He was easy prey to lust because of his fear of rejection and belief that he was unworthy of love. His girlfriend got pregnant when he was seventeen, then she snuck away and had the child aborted. Jonathan's case was a sad one if ever there was. Then, deeply rooted in rejection and already skilled in the art of self-pity, he had his heart broken again by the rich little bitch from the hill. Add onto that, another failed love affair with the Homecoming Queen, and the putrid piece of flesh nearly blew his brains out with a handgun. And we watched and took advantage of every opportunity to bury the slob.

Then he gets filled with HIS SPIRIT and begins to operate under certain gifts doled out by HIM. And then a minister prophesies over the fool that he has the spirit of Elijah upon him and that YOU are against him, which indeed was true. And you succeeded in dashing the boy's spirit when you sent the married strumpet to seduce him — which she did successfully — and he committed his first act of sex with an adulteress. At this point, the fool slinks away, totally defeated, believing himself a hypocrite and even doubting that any of his holy experiences were even real.

He then gets so caught up in the world, that he eventually stops going to church altogether. You make sure he is tightly in the grips of sexual immorality to a point where he falls into nothing less than depravity. You even inspire the women he's with to crave sodomy, and he obliges. He was lost. He was ours. He ended up being addicted to pornography and his sexual desires were running rampant.

But HE wouldn't leave well enough alone. HE had given the boy dreams and those visions never left his mind's eye. And just when the fool was on the verge of being lost forever, the razor blade actually against his pale skin, Raphael descended and chased Asmodeus away once again. Then HE incited that little monkey to invite the miserable finch to that church. And now the fool has found a home.

And once under the shelter of community, the man has made more progress toward his calling in fourteen months than he had in forty years! And, to make matters worse, there is a hedge around him! He's been baptized again! He's operating in the gifts of HIS SPIRIT! His light grows brighter each day!

Jezebel: Please, sire, I have...

Lucifer: QUIET! Give me the rest of your notes.

"Since, then, you have been raised with Christ, set your hearts on things above, where Christ is, seated at the right hand of God. Set your mind on things above, not on earthly

things. For you died, and your life is now hidden with Christ in God" (Colossians 3: 1).

It's clear. He now understands what happened spiritually when he was baptized. You bitch, Jezebel! And this passage is underlined:

"Put to death, therefore, whatever belongs to your earthly nature: sexual immorality, impurity, lust, evil desires and greed, which is idolatry" (Colossians 3: 5).

I can't believe how far we've allowed this to progress. He was lost, but now he is being made new. He's found how to appropriate HIS WORD into reality. He's experiencing the insight that faith in the hearer is the life of the WORD. And look here. Look at this!

"We know that God's children do not make a practice of sinning, for God's Son holds them securely, and the evil one cannot touch them" (1 John 5: 18).

We shall see about this! I'll test his resolve! I'll see how deep his faith has taken root!

Jezebel: But what about the hedge around him, sire? He's already learned the lesson Job learned when you were allowed to persecute him all those centuries ago. Look at the next entry in his notebook.

"My ears had heard of you but now my eyes have seen you" (Job 42: 5).

Lucifer: And here is one last entry in his book:

"Once you were dead because of your disobedience and your many sins. You used to live in sin, just like the rest of the world, obeying the devil – the commander of the powers in the unseen world. He is the spirit at work in the hearts of those who refuse to obey God. All of us used to live that way, following the passionate desires and inclinations of our sinful nature" (Ephesians 2: 1-3).

And here, just under this last passage, you worthless hag, is the death-blow to anything you could have done to him. He has true power against your kind now, you hopeless imp. He has a foundation now against whatever else you could bring against him, for now he has this knowledge in his heart, which is why his light glows so intensely:

"For we are God's masterpiece. He has created us anew in Christ Jesus, so we can do the good things he planned for us long ago" (Ephesians 2: 10).

Jezebel: Please, sire. Surely all is not lost. I have...

Lucifer: No. I'm not even angry any longer. It's all in my hands now.

Jezebel: But sire...

Lucifer: Shush. I went to his church myself, you poor, ignorant failure. I listened to Jonathan as he told his pastor the dream HE gave the man about you. You are worthless to me now. Jonathan has learned how to defeat you. He has learned what needs be done for the dogs to lick up your blood once again. I was there. I listened as Jonathan read the passages to his pastor. And I saw the blueish haze surround him again. And I watched as the pastor received knowledge of Jonathan's calling. The pastor's heart glowed as Jonathan read the verses:

"And also concerning Jezebel the Lord says: 'Dogs will devour Jezebel by the wall of Jezreel.'... There was never a man like Ahab who sold himself to do evil in the eyes of the Lord, urged on by Jezebel his wife" (1 Kings 21: 23 & 25).

And then:

"Then Jehu went to Jezreel. When Jezebel heard about it, she painted her eyes, arranged her hair and looked out of a window...He looked up at the window and called out, 'Who is on my side? Who?' Two or three eunuchs looked down at him. 'Throw her down!' Jehu said. So they threw her down, and some of her blood spattered the wall and the horses as they trampled her underfoot...But when they went out to bury her, they found nothing except her skull, her feet and her hands. They went back and told Jehu, who said, 'This is the word of the Lord that he spoke through his servant Elijah the Tishbite: On the plot of ground at Jezreel dogs will devour Jezebel's flesh'" (2 Kings 30-36).

You poor, silly, wayward wench. Why do you think he's been cloistered? Why do you think a hedge has been placed around him? He's being taught how to destroy you. He's learned the power of fasting and prayer while he's been shut up in that putrid little hotel room he calls home. And there is one truth that not even I have power against. HE has given the man a vision and the man has put his faith in it. And this is one truth you may count certain, for it has forever been so:

"This vision is for a future time. It describes the end, and it will be fulfilled. If it seems slow in coming, wait patiently, for it will surely take place. It will not be delayed" (Habakkuk 2: 3).

I will go now and set my counter attack in order.

Jezebel: But what can you do now, m'lord? What can you do if the man has put his faith in the vision?

Lucifer: Are you entirely daft? Have you not learned anything? Jonathan has the spirit of Elijah upon him. And that means he must needs pass a double portion of his anointing on to one that will succeed him. Do you forget so easily? It is not Elijah who anointed Jehu. Elijah's servant, Elisha, begged for a double portion of the prophet's anointing before Elijah was taken up in the whirlwind. Elisha then anointed Jehu and it was Jehu that witnessed your destruction. Jonathan must pass on a double portion of his anointing to a successor. I shall discover who this successor is. I will lurk in the shadows and I will set snares for the one Jonathan anoints. It is not finished yet. We shall see what comes of it. I shall have my satisfaction, or the successor will restore the family unit and the trumpet blast shall sound.

THE END

NOTES

Parable I

Hosea 12: 10 (New American Standard Bible. The Lockman Foundation. La Habra, CA. 1960).

Numbers 12: 6 (The Holy Bible, New International Version. Zondervan Bible Publishers. Grand Rapids, MI. 1984).

2 Samuel 11: 1 – 12: 4 (New Living Translation. Tyndale House Publishers, Inc. Carol Stream, IL. 1996).

Proverbs 3: 11, 12 (NIV).

Hebrews 12: 10, 11 (NIV).

1 Chronicles 22: 5 – 29: 25 (NLT).

2 Chronicles 1: 7 – 12 (NLT).

1 Kings 9: 2 – 11: 1-3 (NLT).

2 Corinthians 6: 14-16 (NLT).

1 Kings 11: 4-6 (NLT).

1 Corinthians 6: 18, 19 (NLT).

1 Kings 11: 7-10 (NLT).

2 Samuel 7: 12-15 (NIV).

Nehemiah 1: 3 (NIV).

Nehemiah 13: 23-27 (NLT).

Deuteronomy 17: 16, 17 (NIV).

Luke 1: 17-19 (NLT).

1 Kings 6: 29-31 (NLT).

Revelation 2: 18-22 (NIV).

Proverbs 7: 6-27 (NIV).

Matthew 11: 1 (NLT).

1 Kings 3: 16-28 (NLT).

Matthew 12: 22, 23 (NIV).

Jeremiah 32: 35 (NIV).

Isaiah 34: 14, 15 (NLT).

Genesis 6: 1-5 (NLT).

Ephesians 6: 12 (NLT).

2 Corinthians 12: 2-4 (NLT).

Romans 1: 21-32 (NLT).

1 Corinthians 6: 18-20 (NLT).

1. Joseph Campbell, *The Power of Myth* (New York, NY. Bantam Doubleday Dell Publishing Group, Inc. 1988).

2. Nathaniel Hawthorne, *The House of the Seven Gables* (Boston, MA. Tickner & Fields, 1851).

3. Steve Morris, *His Word: A Prophetic Perspective* (www.angelfire.com, 3/4/15).

4. Carl Jung, *Man and His Symbols* (New York, NY. Dell Publishing, 1964).

5. John 3: 5 (NIV).

6. John 4: 24 (NIV).

7. John 16: 13-15 (NIV).

8. John 17: 7 (NIV).

9. Jimmy Joe, Timeless Myths. (www.timelessmyths.com, 1999).

10. Jimmy Joe.

11. Job 36: 21 (NLT).

12. 1 Kings 19: 7 (NLT).

13. J. Gordon Melton, *Encyclopedia of Occultism and Parapsychology* (Farmington Hills, MI. Gale Group, Inc. 2001).

14. Robert Graves and Raphael Patai, *The Hebrew Myths* (New York, NY. Doubleday, 1964).

[15] Graves and Patai.

[16] Rosemary Ellen Guiley, *Encyclopedia of Angels* (New York, NY. Facts on File, Inc. 1996).

[17] Graves and Patai.

[18] Graves and Patai.

[19] Guiley.

[20] Guiley.

[21] *Who Were The Nephilim?* (http://nwcreation.net/nephilim.html, 8/29/12).

[22] Nwcreation.net.

[23] Nwreation.net.

[24] John 3: 5 (NIV).

[25] Matthew 11: 15 (NIV).

[26] Guiley.

[27] Romans 1: 21-23 (NLT).

[28] Romans

[29] Guiley.

[30] Guiley.

[31] Guiley.

[32] Hebrews 13: 2 (NIV).

[33] Hebrews 13: 2 (NIV).

[34] Tobias 2: 10-14 (New Catholic Edition of the Holy Bible, Catholic Book Publishing Co., New York, NY. 1949).

[35] Kahlil Gibran, *The Prophet*, (New York, NY. Alfred A. Knopf, 1923).

[36] Tobias 3: 1-6 (NCE).

[37] Tobias 3: 7-11 (NCE).

[38] Tobias 3: 13-15 (NCE).

[39] Tobias 3: 16-23 (NCE).

[40] Tobias 6: 16, 17 (NCE).

[41] Tobias 12: 16-21 (NCE).

[42] Dave and Tyra Laughlin, (www.newcreation.org, 3/14/15).

Parable II

Revelation 6: 5, 6 (NIV).

1   1 Samuel 1: 3.

2   1 Samuel 1: 11.

3   Luke 2: 49.

4   Romans 8: 19.

5   Robert Bly, *Iron John*, (Boston, MA. Addison-Wesley, 1990).

6   Bly.

7   John 15: 8.

8   Bly.

9   Bly.

10   Bly

11   Bly.

12   Bly.

13   Bly.

14   Revelation 2: 17.

15   Ezekiel 17: 22-24 (NIV).

Parable III

1   William W. Meissner, S.J., *The Oxford Companion to the Bible*, (New York, NY. Oxford University Press, 1993).

2   Meissner.

3   Job 36: 21.

4   Proverbs 30: 8.
     Psalms 22: 16 (NIV).
     Revelation 22: 15 (NIV).
     Genesis 4: 6, 7 (NIV).
     1 John 3: 12 (NLT).
     Galatians 3: 23-25 (NIV).
     1 Thessalonians 4: 3-8 (NIV).

5   C.S. Lewis, *Mere Christianity*, (New York, NY. Macmillan Publishing Co. 1943).
     Proverbs 3: 11, 12 (NIV).

Hebrews 12: 9-11 (NIV).

Romans 8: 28-30 (NIV).

[6] Richard Foster, *Celebration of Discipline*, (New York, NY. Harper Collins Publishing Co. 1978).

[7] Bible Hub, (http://biblehub.com, 2004).

[8] Bible Hub.

[9] Bible Hub.

[10] Bible Hub.

[11] Tom Marshall, *Living in the Freedom of the Spirit*, (Lancaster, England. Sovereign World Ltd. 2001).

[12] Bible Hub.

[13] Bible Hub.

[14] Bible Hub.

[15] Louis Ginsberg, *The Legends of the Jews*, (Philadelphia, PA. The Jewish Publication Society of America, 1909).

[16] Bible Hub.

[17] Franz Delitzsch, *Biblical Commentary on the Book of Job*, (T. & T. Clark, 1869).

[18] Delitzsch.

[19] Delitzsch.

[20] Delitzsch.

[21] Delitzsch.

[22] Bible Hub.

[23] Brother Lawrence, *The Practice of the Presence of God*, (Peabody, MA. Hendrickson Publishers, 2011).

[24] Lawrence.

[25] Lawrence.

[26] Lawrence.

[27] Lawrence.

[28] Francis I. Andersen, *The Oxford Companion to the Bible*.

[29] V. Raymond Edman, *The Disciplines of Life*, (Wheaton, IL. Scripture Press Foundation, 1948).

[30] Galatians 5: 19-21.

31 Galatians 3: 23 - 4: 5.

32 Colossians 2: 11, 12.

33 Colossians 2: 13, 14.

34 Romans 2: 29, 3: 20, 3: 31.

35 Romans 4: 13, 7: 4-6.

36 Romans 6: 16-18.

37 Romans 6: 20-22.

38 Romans 7: 11.

39 Romans 8: 1, 2.

40 Romans 8: 5, 6.

41 1 John 5: 13.

42 1 John 4: 7-10.

43 Og Mandino, *The Choice*, (New York, NY. Random House, 1986).

44 1 Thessalonians 5: 23, 24.

ABOUT THE AUTHOR

Elsa serves in the teaching and healing ministries at Vineyard Church in Kansas City, Missouri. Mr. Papulot has been part of the prophetic ministry in the church for thirty years, working to "turn the hearts of the fathers to their children" (Luke 1:17).

Printed in the United States
By Bookmasters